Dr. Luke Examines Jesus

Want your life changed?

Bill Myers

VICTOR BOOKS

a division of SP Publications, Inc., Wheaton, Illinois

Offices also in Fullerton, California • Whitby, Ontario, Canada • London, England

Library of Congress Catalog Card Number: 78-68856
ISBN: 0-88207-768-6

VICTOR BOOKS
A division of SP Publications, Inc.
P.O. Box 1825 ● Wheaton, IL 60187

To Brenda
my best friend——
and wife.

Dr. Luke Examines Jesus is specially written to help you sharpen your quiet-time skills as you learn about Jesus by studying the Book of Luke.

Dr. Luke Examines Jesus is also designed for group study. A leader's guide with visual aids (SonPower Multiuse Transparency Masters) is available from your local Christian bookstore or from the publisher.

CONTENTS

INTRODUCTION

If I ran out into the street and asked the first girl I met to marry me, she'd probably die laughing. She wouldn't even know me, let alone love me. So how could I change all that? How could we get to know one another and maybe even fall in love?

We'd communicate.

She'd talk, I'd listen. I'd talk, she'd listen. And, if we were right for each other, we might fall in love—*but not till we got to know one another.*

The same is true with Jesus Christ. Asking Him to forgive our sins and inviting Him to be Lord is one thing—the most important thing. But then what?

Well, He asks us to love Him. But that's ridiculous. How can we possibly love somebody we don't know?

Communication Is the Key

We can only get to know God by talking and listening to Him. We talk to Him through prayer, of course, but what about listening? How do we go about that? Sometimes we hear the Lord as we pray, but usually we hear what He has to say by simply reading His letter to us—the Bible.

Have you ever met a person who's gotten tired of God—who no longer loves Him? Whenever I bump into somebody like that I usually ask just one question: "Did you take time every day to get to know Him?" The answer is always the same: no.

7

Of course, it's impossible to love God if you don't know Him very well. And we get to know Him by talking (praying) and listening (reading the Bible).

That's what this book is all about: to help you get to know God—and maybe even come to love Him a little more.

Start out by finding a private place each morning or evening. Then try to spend some quiet time with Him—5, 10, even 15 minutes praising Him, thanking Him, admitting where you failed, making requests, and just generally loving Him. Expressing your love to God doesn't always have to be a verbal thing. Sometimes it can be a song or just a quiet glow directed toward Him.

All of this is to make sure you're plugged in before you begin so you can hear what He wants to teach you. Get to reading the Scripture first, then this book.

And remember, the enemy will do his best to discourage you in every possible way from connecting with your Power Supply. Don't fall for it. If you set aside a little time each day to communicate with the Creator of the universe, if you make it a daily habit for the rest of your life, the power, the joy, and the love you'll experience will be beyond words.

God bless you as you begin or continue in this personal, intimate love relationship.

WEEK 1

What! Another One?

Day 1   *Read Luke 1:1-4*

Why does the Bible have four different versions of the life of Jesus? Couldn't God get all the information into one story? And why do the four Gospels often tell the same story but from four different viewpoints? Do you suppose it took God four different people and four different tries to get it right? If that's the case, then we really can't believe every word in the Bible. Right?

Wrong. Unfortunately, many people come to that conclusion. Yet we read in the Bible that "All Scripture is inspired by God"—not some, not most, but *all* (2 Timothy 3:16).

So what gives?

When four honest people tell the same story, you get the truth, but from four slightly different angles, because each person has his own way of seeing things.

The same is true with the Gospels. God makes certain that the details and facts are accurate but doesn't turn the writers into robots. He writes the truth through each one of them but lets them keep their own personalities, viewpoints, and vocabularies. Matthew is Jewish by birth and uses Old Testament prophecy to prove Jesus is the Messiah—the one Israel has waited so long for. Luke, on the other hand, is a doctor who sees Jesus as *the* Physician who comes to save a sick and diseased world. Both Matthew's and Luke's accounts are correct. By combining all four Gospels, we get a total picture of God the Son.

In these first four verses, we see other important traits of Luke. For instance, we see proof of his honesty. He starts right off by saying that he never knew Jesus personally, that he was not an eyewitness. (Many people would imply that they were Jesus' best friend—that they knew Jesus better than anyone else.) But Luke's not out to impress anyone. He's going to give the facts.

Luke says that he's researched and investigated everything carefully from the beginning—not some things, not most things, but *everything.*

Who could better teach us about Jesus than a man who loves God and insists on the truth? And remember, the Holy Spirit is guiding his writing. And that's quite a team.

Finally, Luke explains why he's writing and why we should read his Gospel: "so that you might know the *exact* truth about the things you have been taught" (Luke 1:4).

An Unusual Birth Announcement

Day 2   *Read Luke 1:5-25*

According to Jewish tradition, there are seven types of men with whom God can refuse to fellowship. At the top of the list is a man whose wife has no children. But we read that Elizabeth and Zacharias were "righteous in the sight of God" (1:6). So what gives? Why has God seemingly forgotten them? Certainly He can see the shame and humiliation they've gone through all these years thanks to their gossipy and judgmental friends. Why has God refused to give them a child? Why no answer to their prayers?

> *God gives us what we need—not what we want: meat instead of candy bars.*

God answers prayers in different ways. Even though His answer is often yes, He sometimes answers no. It's not because He's some sort of heavy-handed dictator, but because He wants to give us what we desperately need—not what we think we want: meat instead of candy bars. God's third answer is, "Yes, but you've got to *wait*. I'll give it to you at the perfect time." This is the case with Zacharias.

One of the highest Jewish honors is given to Zacharias: burning incense in the temple at Jerusalem (1:9). Many priests have waited an entire lifetime for this one great opportunity, and finally the lot falls to Zacharias. There, in front of the altar, serving the Lord and waiting on Him in prayer, his lifelong request is granted. Notice that the Lord doesn't grant Zacharias' desire when he's out there working, struggling, and sweating to make his dream come true. Instead, it comes true as he waits on the Lord in prayer.

By waiting, Zacharias gets the full blessing: a son who will be filled with the Holy Spirit before he is even born. This is quite a thrill considering Israel has had no great prophet for the past 400 years (since the Old Testament was completed). Not only will his son be a great prophet, he'll also be the one to prepare the people for the coming Messiah!

Still Zacharias' faith isn't all that strong. Even though he knows the story of Abraham and Sarah and what God did in their lives, he still doubts and asks for a sign. Gabriel gives him one, but not exactly what he's hoping for: the father-to-be loses his voice till his senior citizen wife gives birth to a son.

Have you ever thought God was deliberately avoiding your prayers?

Have you ever thought God was deliberately avoiding your prayers? Have you ever prayed for something and realized that God was giving you exactly opposite what you'd asked for? We don't always understand how God works, or why. Our feeble minds won't let us. We just have to believe that God, who sees the past, present, and future, has our best interests in mind—even if we can't see them.

That's what it all comes down to: trusting Him, knowing that He'll never let us down—never.

13

Nothing Is Impossible
with God

Not only does God's Son agree to leave His home in heaven (worse than leaving the Bahamas for Antarctica), but He chooses Nazareth of all places—a second-class town despised by any sophisticated Jew.

It's a safe guess that Mary is in her early teens, since that is the marrying age in her culture. So it is to this young woman that Gabriel makes the greatest birth announcement in history: God is paying an extended visit to mankind. Mary's told to name her Son Jesus, which in Hebrew means "The Lord is Salvation." Gabriel also promises her Jesus will be God's Son as well as Messiah, and His kingdom will last forever!

Unlike Zacharias, she doesn't doubt or even ask for a sign. Instead, she simply asks, "How?" Gabriel explains; and then (maybe because she doesn't ask for one), he gives her a special sign: Elizabeth, her aging relative, is already pregnant.

Mary's response is hard to believe. Being an unwed mother didn't help a woman's popularity too much in those days either. And engagements (Mary was engaged to Joseph) were considered much more important than today. They lasted a year and could only be broken off with a divorce. Any fooling around on her part would be considered adultery. Not only would Joseph probably divorce her; but according to the Law, she could face the death penalty (Deuteronomy 22:23-24).

Naturally, she has good cause to be a little nervous. But instead of looking at all the possible life-shattering dangers, Mary keeps her eyes fixed on God's faithful love and, in a sense, simply says, "Yes, have Your way."

The same is true with us. We have to focus our attention entirely on God if we want to walk over our impossible problems. Then, and only then, when our eyes are fixed firmly on Him, will we have the strength to make that simple yet courageous statement, "Yes, have Your way, Lord."

Yes

Mary rushes to Elizabeth's place, about 65 miles away (not exactly an afternoon stroll). When they meet, Elizabeth's unborn baby leaps for joy as Elizabeth is filled with the Holy Spirit and calls Mary the mother of her "Lord." Elizabeth tells Mary how fortunate she is, not because she has done anything on her own, but because she has simply taken God completely at His word and said yes.

Mary agrees but makes sure the glory goes to the right person. She praises God for choosing her, for His love that encourages the humble, and for the fact that what's happening isn't a new plan but the fulfillment of an ancient promise.

Why Not a Zach, Jr.?

When John is born, everybody is pretty excited. But the neighbors can't quite swallow the name. A backyard, over-the-fence conversation may have gone something like this:

"What's with this John stuff? Listen, Zach, don't you know the firstborn is named after the father? That's how we Jews keep the family name going. There's not a single John in your entire family!"

But Zacharias isn't about to make the same mistake twice. He writes in no uncertain terms, *His name is John.* And because of this act of faith, he immediately begins to speak and prophesy about coming events.

There seems to be a clue of some sort here. Zacharias could not speak till his actions said, "Yes, I trust You, Lord." Elizabeth called Mary blessed because Mary said, "Yes, I trust You, Lord."

In contrast, Adam and Eve blew it (and put the world in the mess it's in) because their actions said, "No, we don't trust You, Lord."

How many times a day could we say, "Yes, I trust You"? God promises us love, peace, and protection. "And we know that God causes all things to work together for good to those who love God, to those who are called according to His purpose" (Romans 8:28).

But how many times do we fall for Satan's lies—feeling that if we don't fret, fuss, and worry, whatever we want will not work out for the *very* best? Those are lies. Don't let them trip you up. Instead, claim the truth whether you can see it at this particular moment or not. As Jesus says, "You shall know the truth, and the truth shall make you free" (John 8:32).

17

Trust the Master Artist

Can you imagine what those poor Jewish scholars went through as they studied the prophecies about the birth of the Messiah? In one place they read that Christ would come from Bethlehem (Micah 5:2-4) and in another that He would come from Egypt (Hosea 11:1). They were probably going out of their minds trying to understand these "contradictions" and secretly accusing God (as some people still do) of making a few mistakes now and then. But in the story of Jesus' birth (read also Matthew 1—2), God pulls it all together.

Have you ever stood close to a painting and seen nothing but big, ugly blobs of paint? From there the picture looks like one gigantic, horrible mistake. But as you step back farther from the picture you see how everything fits together, and that terrible ugly spot actually adds to the beauty. It is necessary. We can be so close to our problems, so involved with them, that we can't see the perfect picture God is painting. We may not understand why we have to put up with some big blob of ugly paint in our lives. We may kick. We may accuse God of making a terrible mistake. But He is the Master Artist. He is the one who stands back and sees the whole picture. He knows exactly what is needed to turn us into beautiful works of art. He doesn't make any mistakes in His pictures—our lives. Trust Him. Trust the Master Artist.

18

God? In a Barn?

Can you imagine being born in a barn? Think of the animals, the filth, the smells, the flies, the dusty, scratchy hay, and having a feeding trough, of all things, for a crib! But God, in His infinite love, once again chooses the humblest possible surroundings. No one can accuse Him of not knowing hardships and pain.

Finally, it's not to the kings, or the great intellectuals, or even the celebrities that God sends another birth announcement. Instead, the Creator of the universe first shares His great joy with simple, humble shepherds. (Apparently high positions don't impress Him too much.)

Suddenly the sky splits apart with "a multitude of the heavenly host praising God" and promising peace on earth to those who please Him (2:13). Try buying a birth announcement like that at your local card shop!

Going Up

One reason God gave the Old Testament Law was to show people (then and now) how far they are from God's holiness.

Jesus' birth, however, is God becoming a human to help us understand Him better—we can't possibly understand Him without help. But in order to reach everybody, He went all the way down to our level: the manger, the poor family, and all the rest.

Not only did He choose to come down to the lowest possible level, but He also had to play by His old rules to save those who were trying to make it that way. We see Joseph and Mary following the ceremonial laws of circumcision and purification for their Son. Why? The Bible says that Jesus was "born under the Law in order that He might redeem those under the Law" (Galatians 4:4).

I Thought He Was with You

Day 7   *Read Luke 2:39-52*

At 12, a Jewish boy becomes more responsible for his actions. No longer can he get by with saying, "Hey, I'm just a kid," or "I didn't know any better." Jesus is 12, almost 13, when He goes to the Feast of the Passover with His parents.

Jerusalem is about 65 miles from Nazareth, so after the seven-day festival, Mary and Joseph join a caravan (it's usually safer to travel in a large group) and head for home. As a rule, the women leave earlier in the morning because they walk slower. Then the men leave, and the two groups meet and camp together in the evening. During the journey, Mary probably figures Jesus is with Joseph while Joseph figures He's with her. It's quite a shock when they get together in the evening and discover He isn't with either of them.

They go through the camp looking for Him and then spend three days searching in Jerusalem, hitting all the festival attractions that should interest a boy of Jesus' age. The last place they expect to find Him is in the temple. But there He is, politely listening and asking questions of the top teachers and amazing all of them with His keen insights and answers.

Mary is naturally upset and accuses Jesus of being inconsiderate of His mother and father. Jesus reminds her firmly, but with a loving gentleness, who His Father is. These are the earliest words of Jesus quoted in the New Testament. Jesus knows why He's visiting earth.

Before this time, no one had ever used the term "My Father" as Jesus has just done. It was always "our Father" or "my Father in heaven." No one has ever referred to God in such a personal, intimate way before.

Even at this age, Jesus knows exactly who He is. Yet He returns with His parents and remains obedient to them. The fact that He is God's Son doesn't give Him special rights to rebel or to disobey.

Another Reminder

Make sure you read the Scripture first and dwell on it, letting the Holy Spirit reveal what He wishes to show you.

Don't rely on this commentary to do the teaching. That's the Holy Spirit's job. Let Him do it as you read and reread the Scripture daily.

Only when you're sure He's finished should you go to the commentary for any further insights He may wish to reveal to you.

WEEK 2

T or F—Circle One

Day 1   *Read Luke 3:1-17*

Once again we find our doctor friend getting into the nitty-gritty details. We see that Luke is not telling us some sort of "once upon a time" fairy tale. Instead, he's careful to give facts which can be proven through Scripture and other historical writings.

Years have passed since the last chapter. Zach's boy is now about 30 years old and living in the wild areas of Judea. God has given him the gift of prophecy; and he is, just as Isaiah had promised centuries before, the one who'll begin preparing people for the coming of Christ.

> *So many people are into "churchianity" instead of a personal relationship with Jesus.*

John's message is fairly simple: Get your act together! Stop doing the things you know are wrong and repent! Get baptized!

But he doesn't stop there. He sees a lot of people faking their religion. He calls them a "brood of vipers" (3:7) and accuses them of going through the outward actions without really being sincere on the inside—where it counts.

It's sad that the same things happen today. So many people are into "churchianity" instead of a personal relationship with Jesus. They go through the outward actions without ever letting Jesus come into their lives and take control.

You Tell 'Em, John

John tells the people they're out in left field if they think they can get by because they're sons of Abraham. Today many of us figure we can get by because we live a good life, glance at the Bible occasionally, or go to church. We've got it made, right? Wrong. Again, only by letting Jesus be our Lord, admitting our shortcomings to Him, and asking Him to take complete control, will we make it. Christ will separate the useful from the useless, those who are sincere from those going along for the ride.

John encourages the people to love others. He also lets them know that he is definitely not the Christ the prophets told about. He can baptize only with water, but the Christ will baptize with the Holy Spirit and with fire. The Holy Spirit will comfort and give us power to do right; the fire will make us pure and clean.

25

Down by the Riverside

Day 2   *Read Luke 3:18-38*

King Herod has divorced his wife and started living with his brother's wife. Obviously God isn't too thrilled with this arrangement, and John points it out. It would have been much safer for John to keep quiet and not mention the problem at all, but that's not real love. Sometimes love is telling a person what he needs to hear, not what he wants to hear.

Even Herod is given the chance to change his ways and say yes to God. But he chooses not to. Instead Herod has John thrown in prison and later has his head chopped off.

But wait a minute! Why is God letting this happen to John? Is this his payment for obedience? Saying yes to God doesn't automatically make situations easier. But God promises to give us a supernatural overflow of peace, joy, and love to get us through any problem—if we let Him. Situations aren't always peachy, but our lives can be full of meaning no matter what.

Why Should Jesus Be Baptized?
We continue to see that Jesus, who is to be the perfect Sacrifice for our sins, stays free from sin. Then why does He get baptized if He's already perfect? Just as He does with the ancient ceremonial laws, Jesus again follows the rules in order to live the perfect life.

After the baptism and prayer, we see for the first time since Creation, the three Persons of God together

26

at one time: the Son (Jesus), the Spirit (in the form of a dove), and the Father (the voice). And now for the obvious question: "How can one God be in three forms?"

That's a biggie. It's a question that's given man headaches for centuries, because of his limited capacity to comprehend. One good way to understand God is by looking at man. A man can be a son (to his parents), a father (to his children), and a husband (to his wife). He's all three things at once, and still he's one person. We have one God, but He is three Persons.

Another way of tackling this question is by taking a close look at water. Even though it can be found in three separate forms—ice, water, steam—it will always remain "water."

The same is true of God. He is one God and will always remain one God. Yet He exists in three different forms.

A Handbook for Victory

Read Luke 4:1-12

If Jesus slips up just once, commits even one little sin, it's all over. God will no longer have the perfect Sacrifice to live and die in our place—the world cannot be saved. Satan also knows this. So he uses all of his strength and cunning to get Jesus to stumble just once.

It's been 40 days and nights in the wilderness with no food. That's nearly six weeks! Naturally, Jesus is hungry. And Satan is there with his first phase of attack: the temptation of immediate self-gratification.

"Tell this stone to become bread," he tells Jesus (4:3). Satisfy your physical desires, in other words. Let those desires have control! Why wait for marriage to have sex? Why turn down that joint? Why refuse that extra piece of pie? If it feels good, do it! Sound familiar?

This trick fails, so Satan goes into phase 2: "If You will worship before me, [the world] shall all be Yours" (4:7). If we compromise, we'll have it made. One lie, and the business deal is ours. If we cheat a little, we'll get good grades.

He tempts Christ a second time. Say no to God just this once, and You'll get all this *plus* the glory for Yourself.

But Satan fails again. Finally, he makes a desperate attempt. He taunts Jesus by trying to get Him to prove He's God's Son.

Does Satan ever ask you: "Are you sure God really

loves you? Are you sure you're special to Him? Has He proved it lately?"

Satan attacks Jesus hard and heavy (fighting for the very world); and each time, a physically exhausted Jesus wins. How? What's His secret?

There's definite supernatural power in the Word of God.

First, Jesus is filled with the Holy Spirit. But there's more. He doesn't try to resist the attack by Himself. Instead He relies on Scripture.

There's definite supernatural power in the Word of God. The Book of Ephesians lists the things we're to wear when we go into battle against the enemy. Most of the items are defensive. We're given the only *offensive* weapon we need, "the sword of the Spirit which is the *Word of God*" (Ephesians 6:17).

Madman or God?

Day 4   *Read Luke 4:13-21*

Satan leaves Jesus after failing to tempt Him. But he's not gone forever. Again and again throughout Jesus' life, Satan returns and tries to pressure Him into slipping. It's encouraging to know that Jesus goes through it all. He understands how difficult resisting temptation is. He can sympathize with our weakness because He "has been tempted in all things as we are" (Hebrews 4:15).

Jesus doesn't stay away from sin because of some secret supernatural power that only He has. No, that wouldn't be playing fair. Jesus is limited to the same resources we have today—the Word and the Spirit. We've briefly mentioned the power of the Word, but what about the power of the Holy Spirit?

Before Jesus leaves His disciples, He promises to send Someone—the Holy Spirit—to help them till He returns. It is the Holy Spirit who gives the disciples the power to heal and raise people from the dead. This same Person lives inside every believer. This is the Person who helps us grow as Christians and resist temptation—if we allow Him to have His way in our lives.

After the series of temptations, Jesus returns to Galilee "in the power of the Spirit" (4:14). He quickly begins to make quite a name for Himself and is "praised by all" (4:15).

When Jesus arrives at His hometown and stands up

to read in the synagogue (not an uncommon custom back then), He makes it clear that He is more than some goody-goody teacher. Jesus reads one of the more than 300 prophecies that promise a Saviour, and says, "Today this Scripture has been fulfilled" (4:21). He is openly claiming to be the Messiah!

Jesus is either the world's greatest liar, a madman, or who He says He is—God.

It would be nice to write Jesus off as some kind of smooth teacher and then forget Him. But He doesn't allow that. Over and over in the New Testament He says, in effect, "Hey, it's Me, God the Son. I'm God."

C. S. Lewis hit it right on when he said that Jesus Christ can only be one of three kinds of men: the world's greatest liar, a madman, or exactly who He says He is—God the Son. But nobody can call Him just a "smooth teacher." He doesn't leave us that option.

I Remember You When . . .

At first everyone seems to like Jesus. But soon the ol' pride sets in, and people begin muttering such things as, "Isn't this Joseph's son?"

This could be translated: "Hey, who do you think you are? I knew you when you were just a kid and your old man and I used to share rides on each other's camels," or "Listen, friend, I was playing first string guard on the Nazareth team while you sat warming the bench. So don't come on with this 'Messiah' stuff."

Though these aren't their exact words, Jesus knows that this is what His old acquaintances are thinking: *If you're the Messiah, prove it. Give us a sign, like in Capernaum when you chased a demon out of that guy. You owe it to your hometown buddies!*

This attitude isn't quite right. First, it reeks with pride. And second, it fails to realize that God isn't about to be forced into proving Himself for anyone or anything. He's not a carnival magician who wows the crowd with sideshow acts. That's not His style. God uses signs and miracles to reach out in love to people. He doesn't perform tricks.

Jesus points out the pride problem by mentioning two Old Testament accounts. In both cases the Jewish people refused to accept their own prophets, and God responded by sending those prophets to foreigners. Both times God wouldn't help His chosen people because of their pride.

These reminders don't go over too well in the Jewish synagogue. Jewish people are supposed to be God's favorites. As far as they are concerned, the foreigners—the other nations—exist only to keep the fires of hell burning, so to speak. These Israelites aren't too happy when this young upstart tramples all over their pride—and without cleaning his sandals first either.

So they escort Jesus from the city to the edge of a nearby cliff. But this is neither the time nor place for Jesus to die. Much more has to be done. So for the first time in the Book of Luke, Jesus seems to use His supernatural powers.

The Bible doesn't elaborate: One moment an angry mob holds Jesus over the edge of a cliff. The next moment, the "helpless victim" has vanished.

Even Demons Believe

Jesus leaves His hometown and travels to the city of Capernaum on the shore of the Sea of Galilee, a journey of about 20 miles.

At this time in history, Jewish teachers are taking great care not to say anything original. When they teach, they always use quotes from the past. They repeat, "So and so said this, or so and so said that," but never say anything on their own authority.

Suddenly Jesus comes along saying, "Truly *I* say to you," and "*I* tell you this." Everyone is pretty much blown away by the authority He speaks with.

Not only does He dazzle the religious bigwigs with His authority, He even drives out demons. The synagogue is a place for teaching and quiet, reverent worship; but today the silence is shattered by the screams of a demon-possessed man. The different demons in the man recognize Jesus as "the Holy One of God" and cry out, wanting to know if He has come to destroy them. (Apparently one demon speaks for all of them.)

Even the demons (angels thrown out of heaven with Satan) know that Jesus is God the Son. Yet they are not saved from their sins, because they don't depend on Jesus to save them. Today some people cruise through life, believing Jesus is the Son of God; but that's where their belief stops. That's not enough! "The demons also believe, and shudder" (James 2:19). The key is to count on Jesus to forgive your sin, and then let Him call the shots and sit at the control panel of your life. He's either your Boss or He isn't.

Jesus doesn't go through any hocus-pocus—no dangling crosses, fancy chants, or magical spells. He gets right to the point and simply but firmly tells the demon to be quiet and get out. Today it's still the power and authority of Jesus Christ through the Holy Spirit that accomplishes miracles—nothing else—no fancy words or great personalities—simply Jesus Christ.

The demons make a fast exit.

There will be no lack of conversation at the dinner tables in Capernaum tonight. All are wondering, *Who is this Messenger of God?*

A Long Day

After all the pressures of preaching on Sunday, most pastors return home exhausted. The same is probably true of Jesus. After teaching and healing at the synagogue, He is probably looking forward to some rest and relaxation at Simon's house (4:38).

But Simon Peter's mother-in-law is sick with a high fever. Without hesitation, Jesus cures her. The healing is so extensive, so complete, that she doesn't even need to rest and recuperate. The loss of energy that always comes from a high fever is miraculously missing. Immediately she's on her feet, serving them!

There's another lesson here: She could start telling everyone that God chose her for a healing. After all, He did choose her, didn't He?

But she doesn't go on any talk shows or write a book about the miracle. Instead she uses God's gift as He intends her to use it. She gets up and starts serving others.

At this time in history, Jewish tradition says that carrying a sick man on the Sabbath is work; and no work is to be done on the Sabbath. So as soon as the sun goes down (ending the Sabbath), there's a mad rush to Peter's house. Jesus decides to work on into the night healing "every one" of the sick (4:40). That's love.

More demons recognize Jesus as the Son of God, but He silences them "because they [know] Him to be the Christ" (4:41). Why? Why does He keep that fact hidden sometimes?

Two types of Bible prophecies spoke of the Messiah. One told of a political Liberator who was to free the world from its bondage. The other spoke of a suffering Saviour who would die for humanity's sins. Not realizing the job was to be done in two phases (Jesus dying to save and later returning to rule), the Jews concentrate only on the political prophecies. Jesus knows this and fears that the people might try to set Him up as king—their political hero. So, for the time being at least, He occasionally hides His identity.

In the morning Jesus leaves to find a quiet place. The Gospels of Matthew and Mark explain that Jesus does this so He can pray and be with the Father. Even Jesus takes time in the morning to find a quiet place and to worship God.

WEEK 3

Go for the Long Shot

Day 1   *Read Luke 5:1-16*

Peter and his partners have had a long, frustrating night. Despite all their hard work and long hours, they haven't caught a fish. Numb with exhaustion, they begin the tedious job of cleaning their nets, looking forward to collapsing in their own beds at home.

But Jesus comes along and asks Peter to let Him use his boat as a speaker's platform.

When Jesus finishes speaking, He tells Peter to go back out and fish again.

What! Doesn't this new Teacher realize that broad daylight is the worst possible time in the world to fish with nets? If we couldn't catch anything at night when conditions were the best, how can we possibly catch anything now?

No doubt these thoughts are racing through Peter's mind. But he goes for the long shot and says yes to Jesus, despite the odds. The results are miraculous only because Peter is willing to say yes to God even when all the circumstances say no.

After seeing the incredible catch that nearly sinks his boat, Peter falls down at Jesus' feet and calls Him

"Lord." Peter says he is unworthy even to be near Jesus and asks Him to leave. But Jesus tells him not to be afraid, because from now on he'll be catching men's souls instead of fish. Later, when Peter, John, and James get back to shore, they leave everything and follow Jesus.

Leprosy: A Lonely Disease

At this time leprosy is considered to be living death. The disease starts with a small spot on the skin and spreads till arms, legs, and whole parts of the body literally begin to rot away. Since leprosy is contagious, the leper must live by himself, completely cut off from everyone else. If people accidently approach him, the leper must shout, "Unclean, unclean!" It's a lonely, humiliating life.

Yet Jesus breaks all of the social rules with the big one: love. A leper sneaks into the city and timidly approaches Jesus. People are probably terrified, pushing and shoving to get out of his way, afraid he might accidently brush against one of them. But what does Jesus do? In that infinite love of His, He actually reaches out and touches the rotting flesh. The man is made well immediately.

Again we see God the Son slipping away to a quiet spot to pray.

Who Does He Think He Is?

Jesus is getting to be quite a celebrity. Scribes and Pharisees are coming from all parts of Israel to see Him in person. Scribes are men who spend their entire lives defining and redefining every detail of the Law. Pharisees are religious leaders who set themselves apart from everyone else by trying to follow all those details. Both scribes and Pharisees are usually trying to follow the Law so closely they forget the purpose of it. With them, Law comes first. They're about to see that with God, love comes first.

The house where Jesus is teaching is so packed that a paralyzed man can't even get through the door. His friends strain and struggle to get him on the roof, then tear a hole in it and lower him in front of Jesus.

Jesus sees the man's tremendous faith and says, "Friend, your sins are forgiven you" (5:20).

But the scribes and Pharisees explode. "What! Who does He think He is—God? Only God can forgive sins!"

Jesus lets them know that's exactly who He is: "The Son of Man has authority on earth to forgive sins" (5:24). ("Son of Man" was the term an Old Testament prophet used in referring to the Messiah.)

Jesus sees a connection between sickness and sin. A man comes to Him to be healed; and the first thing Jesus does is to cleanse him of his sins, something he hadn't even asked for.

Jesus takes care of the man's greatest sickness first, his sins. Jesus then emphasizes His point by completing the healing: "I say to you, rise" (5:24).

The man does just that and everyone is "seized with astonishment" as the man picks up his bed and heads for home, glorifying God (5:26).

IF THE SCRIBES CAN'T FIND A LAW FOR SOMETHING, THEY MAKE ONE UP.

"THOU SHALT NOT LAUGH WHEN TICKLED."

"THOU SHALT NOT USE THY FEET WHEN WALKING OR THY HANDS WHEN EATING."

"THOU SHALT NOT PERSPIRE ON FRIDAY AFTERNOONS."

"THOU SHALT NOT CRY AT

Throw Out the Old

Day 3   *Read Luke 5:27-39*

Jewish tax collectors often bribe the Roman government for the opportunity to collect taxes. They make a
tremendous profit by cheating and overtaxing their
neighbors. Consequently tax collectors aren't too
popular. The Jewish people put them in the same
class as robbers and murderers and won't even let
them enter the synagogue. Yet Jesus approaches
Levi, a tax collector, and says, "Follow Me."

It's not up to us to judge who'll come to God and
who won't. Sometimes the least likely are the first to
follow—maybe even become superleaders. (Levi, also
called Matthew, later will become one of the Twelve
Apostles and write the Gospel of Matthew.) Only God
knows people's hearts. Our job is to "preach the
Gospel to all creation" (Mark 16:15)—not to judge.

Matthew leaves *everything* behind to follow Jesus.
He doesn't try to add Jesus to his life (like adding a
new patch to rotting jeans). Instead he completely
replaces his rags with a brand new pair. If we receive
Jesus, we don't add Him to our life to fix it up. Instead, we let Him throw the old life away so there's
room for the new one—His.

As Jesus eats with the tax collectors, the scribes and
Pharisees complain that He's associating with "sinners." But Jesus lets them know that sin is a sickness and He has come to save the sick. That's not to
say He thinks the scribes are well. (Later, He has a

meal with them.) But Matthew's friends know they are sick. Jesus knows it's much easier for a doctor to help those who know they're ill than to heal those who refuse to believe there's anything wrong with them.

Again, He points out the need for people to let Him throw out the old life. It does no good to sew a new patch on rags. It does no good to simply add Jesus to our lives—to receive Him and continue chasing after the world. We should be willing to let Him throw out the old and replace it with His new.

TAX COLLECTORS AREN'T THE BEST FRIENDS TO HAVE AROUND. BUT THAT DIDN'T STOP JESUS.

Help for God

God doesn't force anyone to accept His gift of eternal life. That decision is always ours. He never sends anyone to hell. We alone make that decision. After hearing the Gospel we choose our final destination. And as painful as it may be to Him, God always honors our decision, our freedom of choice.

Still, in that incredible love of His, He continually offers the gift. He waits for us with a big smile on His face and His arms open wide. That's some love.

For those who have decided to follow God, the trip is incredible: going places we never dreamed possible, seeing things we've never imagined. Granted, we may go through rains, blizzards, and storms; but as long as we stay under His protection, we'll get by.

God is love, not lists of rules.

Sometimes the road gets bumpy—real bumpy. We have to trust Him completely, resisting the temptation of breaking away and trying to go it alone. Relax and trust Him. He knows what He's doing.

Sometimes we think we can help Him be a better God. That's ridiculous.

Yet that's what the Pharisees are doing, inventing thousands of additions to God's Law to try to make themselves more holy. The trouble is, they've been doing it so long that they've forgotten what it was like to let God run the show.

Again we see Jesus reminding them that God is love, not lists and lists of rules.

But they ignore this main issue and complain that He is not playing the Sabbath by their rules. Jesus sets them straight (6:5). In a sense He's asking, "You're going to tell Me, the Creator of the Sabbath, what to do on the Sabbath?"

A Talk with the Boys

Jesus makes an important decision. Who will be His apostles? Who will be His inner circle of close friends that will spread the Gospel after He leaves? Instead of relying on charts, figures, and computers, Jesus spends an entire night praying alone to the Father.

He names the Twelve Disciples. They're just ordinary men with different backgrounds. Some are even bitter enemies. (Matthew, the tax collector, is considered a traitor to his country, while Simon the Zealot belongs to an organization that swears to kill all traitors.) The men make an interesting combination, but the love of Jesus breaks down all barriers and teaches them to work with one another and love one another.

Jesus now begins His famous Sermon on the Mount, considered by many scholars to be some of the greatest teaching in the history of the world.* As we study it these next three sessions, also read Matthew 5—7 a couple times—slowly. Allow the Holy Spirit to reveal deeper and deeper layers of truth to you.

Jesus begins by saying how blessed we are if we're poor, hungry, weeping, and even hated because of Jesus. In fact, He says, "Be glad . . . and leap for joy" if we're insulted because of Him (6:23). If we're really letting Jesus be Lord, our rewards won't always come through outward situations. But we can have the peace, the love, and the joy of the Holy Spirit bubbling up and overflowing inside us, something no amount of money can buy.

On the other hand, if we're still chasing after the world, its riches, its superficial happiness and fame, we may get what we want. But that's all. There'll be no eternal life and no inner peace. In fact, Jesus says such people will be unhappy. Not only will they miss out on a super eternity (after their brief stay on earth); but, after the fun wears off, the things they worked for will lose their meaning anyway.

Remember how much we wanted something for Christmas when we were younger? Whatever we got was fun—for a while. But as the weeks passed, we got bored and wanted something else. The same is still true, whether the goody is a yo-yo or an expensive sports car. Nothing can possibly fill that empty space in our hearts that was especially designed for God to fill—except God.

---

*For a closer look at Jesus' teachings on the Sermon on the Mount, read *Life: Jesus-Style* by James Long, another SonPower elective.

My Shirt Too!

Day 6   *Read Luke 6:27-38*

The truths in these verses are so important, so necessary for us to remember in our everyday lives. After looking at each verse and chewing on it thoroughly, let's put ourselves in each of those situations. See how they apply to what we're going through today.

Jesus is speaking of love—not the gushy sentimentality that people manufacture, package, and sell, but the firm, active, selfless love that can come only from God.

A love for those who hate us.

A love that causes us to bless and even pray for those who mistreat us.

A love that is concerned for others.

A love that gives without expecting anything in return.

Before Jesus comes on the scene, the great "religious" saying of the time was, "Don't do anything to anybody that you wouldn't want them to do to you." But Jesus indicates that doing to others is only the beginning. We are to *do* to others what we want them to do us. But we're not supposed to be thinking what we can get out of the deal.

We are to become just as merciful as our Father.

We are not to pass judgment or condemn, but forgive and pardon—and we'll be forgiven and pardoned.

If we give, it will be given back to us with interest.

All of these thoughts show God's love. And if they all sound impossible to live by, you're right. Only God can live by them, because only He has a love like that. But as we submit to Him, as we continue to allow Him to be the Boss, we slowly find that we can begin to do those things, not because we have to, but because we want to.

Don't forget to read Matthew 5—7. (See yesterday's session.)

Condensed Food

Day 7   *Read Luke 6:39-49*

Jesus has so much to say, so much to do while He's here on earth. There are so many things that the Creator has to say about His creation. In fact, after writing an entire book on Jesus, the Apostle John ends with: "And there are also many other things which Jesus did, which if they were written in detail, I suppose that even the world itself would not contain the books which were written" (John 21:25).

This may also be the case here with Luke. He has so much to record that he has to abruptly end one point and begin another to get it all in. In this brief passage for today we see four major topics.

In the first couple verses, Jesus warns people to stay away from the Pharisees. They're blind, He says. If we follow blind guides we fall into holes in the ground. But if we follow Jesus, He promises to lead us to eternal life.

Then Jesus reminds us with a humorous illustration to get our acts together before we start trying to clean up other people's.

He also says we do what we are (6:43-45). If we're a lemon tree (if we haven't let Jesus come in and begin changing us), try as we might on our own to grow peaches, we'll grow lemons. Oh sure, we can fake it for a while and look as if we're growing peaches—you know, paint our fruit and glue some fur on the outside. We may even fool ourselves for a while. But as soon

NO MATTER HOW HARD IT TRIES, A LEMON CAN NEVER BECOME A PEACH.

as someone takes a bite, he gets lemon (plus a mouthful of fur).

On the other hand, a peach tree can only bear peaches. It can't help it. It doesn't strain or strive. The fruit just comes out that way.

Finally Jesus tells us to build our houses with firm foundations in Him, not like those of the people who go for the quick payoff. Sand castles may look great and are a snap to build, but they're short-term investments. One rain or big wave, and it's all over. Jesus encourages us to build on His rock, His firm foundation, with materials that will last.

WEEK 4

Healing by Long Distance

Day 1   *Read Luke 7:1-10*

At this time the Romans and Jews hate each other.
For about a hundred years Israel has been occupied by
the Roman army. At the heart of that army are the
centurions. They are the commanders—usually harsh,
brutal men representing the strong fist of Rome.

But here we see a different type—a centurion who
shows compassion. Slaves at this time are considered
nothing more than pieces of property. When they
cease to function properly, they're thrown away like
broken tools and replaced by new ones. Yet this centurion shows a great concern for his slave.

The usual Roman-Jewish hatred doesn't seem to
exist between this centurion and his Jewish slave. The
Roman has even helped build a Jewish synagogue.

And now the Jewish elders approach Jesus and say
that this Roman centurion is "worthy" (7:4), quite a
statement to make about the enemy.

The strict religious Jews of this time never enter a
Gentile's house. Yet without hesitation Jesus heads
for the centurion's place. But as He approaches the
house, the centurion sends his friends out to Him with

the message, "I am not fit for You to come under my roof . . . but just say the word, and my servant will be healed" (7:6-7).

This is the only time in the entire New Testament that Jesus "marvels" at someone's faith. He turns to the crowd and says, "Not even in Israel have I found such great faith" (7:9).

And a great faith it is. We can learn a lot from this man's simple, absolute faith. This is the childlike faith Jesus encourages us all to have: *God says it, I believe it, that settles it.*

But simple faith is not something we can manufacture on our own or buy at the local Christian bookstore. Such faith can only come from God as we continue to know Him better, grow to love Him, and yield to Him.

"I Say to You, Arise!"

Day 2   *Read Luke 7:11-17*

A crowd follows Jesus as He travels from Capernaum to Nain, about a day's walk. As they approach the city gate, Jesus and the crowd are met by another crowd heading for the local graveyard.

The funeral is a loud affair. Professional mourners have been hired and they lead the procession, clanging cymbals, playing flutes, and wailing. The mother walks alone behind this sad group. The coffin containing her dead son follows behind.

A mother losing her only child is a painful thought. But we read that this woman's husband is also dead. This means she's now completely alone. Whom will she turn to? How will she survive? Who can possibly comfort her now? Her heartache and misery must be unbearable.

As Jesus' eyes meet hers He is filled with compassion. It's comforting to know that as we go through heartache, pain, and suffering, Jesus is right there by our side, feeling every tear, every ache, every bit of sorrow.

But Jesus does more than feel sad in this instance. He stops the procession and exercises His authority over death.

Today, thousands of people who are trying the Eastern philosophies and the "you too can improve yourself" religions overlook the fact that Jesus is the only "Teacher" who has authority over death. Other philosophers may have catchy slogans or ideas, but when it comes to death they're powerless. Yet in just three years Jesus exercises His power over death at least four times!

When the Antichrist comes, he'll be able to fake some of this power through trickery, but only Jesus has the real authority.

It's interesting that Jesus doesn't say, "In the name of God, arise." Instead He proves once again that He is God with the words, "*I* say to you, arise!" (7:14)

The man rises up and begins talking. All are amazed at Jesus' display of power, and they begin calling Him a Prophet. Well, they're getting closer.

Just Ask Me, I'll Show You

Day 3   *Read Luke 7:18-35*

John the Baptist has lived in the wide open spaces all his life. He now finds himself rotting in the dark hole of a prison. Because he's a man, he has a man's fears and doubts. Being tossed into a dungeon isn't exactly what he had hoped for. Maybe he's made a mistake about Jesus. Maybe Jesus isn't the Messiah after all. To make sure, John sends two friends to ask Jesus who He really is.

The Lord understands John's doubts and doesn't scold him. Instead, He answers John's question in much the same way He answers the questions of those who are honestly searching today: "Listen to what I have said, and look at all I have done."

As the messengers leave, Jesus turns to the people and says that John is the man whom the prophets said would prepare the way for the Messiah. No man is greater than John. Still the "least in the kingdom of God is greater than he" (7:28). Even though John loves God and has sacrificed a lot for Him, he still isn't perfect.

But if we've become a part of the kingdom of God, He sees us as perfect, as being better than John—not because of what we've done, but because of what Jesus did for us.

A Million Is a Million

A man is eating dinner with his friends. Suddenly a woman rushes in and begins kissing his feet and wiping them with her hair. Naturally you'd think he'd be a little embarrassed and try to stop her. But in this case the Man is Jesus, and He sees past this woman's actions to her needs. Here is an "immoral woman" who is trying desperately to find some way to humble herself before God—to say she's sorry for the life she's been living and to ask Him to forgive her. Though her actions may seem inappropriate, she humbles herself in the only manner she knows. And Jesus understands completely.

Sin is sin. Whether it's 5 sins or 5 million really makes little difference.

Simon the Pharisee, on the other hand, doesn't understand and is going out of his mind. Here he is, trying to carry on a nice dinner conversation with his guest while this woman off the streets is pouring oil all over Jesus' feet, kissing them, and crying. Old Simon is pretty uptight with the whole thing. He figures Jesus isn't a prophet or He'd know this woman was immoral and tell her to leave.

Jesus knows what's going on inside Simon's mind

and asks a simple question: "If a person owes a man 50 days' worth of daily wages and another owes 500 days' worth of wages, and the man forgives them both, who would love him more?"

The answer, of course, is the person who is forgiven the most.

Jesus agrees and points out the same is true with sin. In the Bible we read, "All have sinned and fall short of the glory of God" (Romans 3:23). We're all in debt and guilty. It's not a matter of how much we owe—whether it's $5 or $5 million.

People who have lived good lives often lose what the Bible calls that "first love" for God (Revelation 2:4). They figure they owe God less and are often less grateful than people who have been deeply into sin and forgiven.

Sin is sin. Whether it's 5 sins or 5 million really makes little difference. Jesus died for each of our sins, in our place, so we can have that perfect friendship with God. That's what makes the difference.

Let's Let Him Shine

Jesus begins visiting various cities and villages, "proclaiming and preaching the kingdom of God" (8:1). He has His twelve disciples with Him as well as several women who help support Jesus' ministry.

After He teaches a complicated parable to a large group of people, His disciples ask Him to clarify it. He explains that He uses parables so only His serious followers will understand the "mysteries of the kingdom" (8:10). That's not to say He's trying to hide His plan of salvation—not by any means! But rather He intends that the deeper meanings and truths be only for His fully dedicated children.

In the parable He just told, the seed is the Word of God that sometimes falls on packed-down ground. Many people are like that ground. They're so hardened and calloused that their pride won't let them listen to anyone.

A second group of people is like the rocky soil (rocks with a thin layer of dirt over them). They're told about Jesus and begin to grow—often quickly. But they have no roots. They haven't taken the time to get to know God personally. So when the sun comes up and beats down on them, when things get rough, they quit. (The sad thing is these same rough times are what God uses to encourage people to sink their roots deeper into Him.)

Finally there is the good soil: the people who hear

the Word and stay with the truth through trials and hardships.

After this, Jesus encourages His followers to let His Light shine through them.

If we have received Jesus, we have the very Light of heaven inside us. If we're to bring light into a dark world, we can't hide or cover it. Let's let Him shine.

Finally, Jesus mentions that there is no standing still in the Christian walk. We're either moving forward or sliding backward. We can't just "get by." We either continue to shine God's light or lose it. There's no in between.

Go and Tell

Jesus is not rejecting His earthly family when He says anyone who obeys the Word of God is part of His family. He loves His family dearly. In fact, one of the last things He does while on the cross is to make sure His mother is looked after. Jesus is saying that you and I are just as important to Him as His own mother *if we hear the Word of God and act according to it.*

> **Jesus isn't some disinterested god way out there somewhere.**

Jesus has been teaching all that day and is probably pretty beat. He falls asleep in the boat as His followers and He cross the Sea of Galilee. The storm that comes up must be pretty big, since it causes fishermen who have weathered many storms to panic. They figure they can't handle this one and wake Jesus, yelling, "We're going to die! We're going to die!"

Jesus wakes and simply tells the wind and waves to be quiet. Suddenly everything calms down. After all, what could be more natural than the Creator of all things (see John 1:3, 10) controlling all things?

By this action Jesus is not only beginning to reveal who He is but also that God can and will always take care of us—even if conditions look impossible.

61

When they arrive on shore, Jesus and His disciples meet a demon-possessed man who has been running around naked and living in tombs. The demons recognize Jesus as being the Son of God and beg Him not to cast them into the pit of hell. Jesus commands them to leave the man but allows them to enter a herd of pigs. The demon-possessed pigs then take a leap off a cliff.

After realizing what has happened, the people of the area ask Jesus to leave. They seem more concerned about losing the pigs than that a man is healed.

Once again we see that God is a Gentleman. He's been asked to leave; He will leave. As He turns to go, the healed man begs to come along. But Jesus tells him to remain behind and tell others what God has done for him.

The same is true with us. We're not immediately whisked up into heaven to be with Jesus when we receive Him. He wants us to stay here and tell others.

"Just You and Me"

As Jesus returns, He finds a big crowd waiting for Him. And in that crowd is a synagogue official, one of the most respected and admired men in the village. But right now that doesn't make much difference to him because his only daughter is dying. This highly respected man throws himself at Jesus' feet in front of everybody, begging for Jesus to come to his house.

But before Jesus raises the girl from her sleep (sleep is a term used in the New Testament to describe a believer's death), there is another matter to attend to.

In the midst of that tightly packed crowd is another person who desperately needs Jesus' help—a woman who can't stop her bleeding. Because of her problem, she is not only forbidden to worship in the temple, but she isn't even allowed to touch another living person—and this has been going on for 12 years!

She pushes through the crowd and manages to touch just the fringe of Jesus' clothes. Immediately she's healed.

But there in the middle of the crowd, Jesus stops and asks who touched Him. Peter thinks the question is a little strange, since so many people are pushing in from all sides. Yet Jesus insists that the person be identified. It's not because He needs to know who she is, but He wants to personally reach out to her even in the middle of a huge, shoving crowd.

Today Jesus is still reaching out to each of us individually, saying, "Hey, it's just you and Me. In the middle of this huge crowd I'm with you every second. Others may know you only as a number, but to Me you're an important person."

Sometimes this is difficult to believe since there are billions of other people in the world. But we're finite; we can only be in one place at one time. Remember, God is infinite; He is in all places at all times. And He is always, day and night, right there by our side saying, "Hey, let's walk together—just you and Me."

WEEK 5

Give the Gift

Day 1   *Read Luke 9:1-17*

Jesus calls His twelve together and gives them authority over demons as well as power to heal. But they're not given those special abilities for their own use—oh no. They're given those powers to help comfort others and to help spread the Gospel.

God has given each of us Christians special gifts and abilities—not for our own benefit but for the benefit of others

"Now hold it," you might say. "I don't have a special gift. I can't do anything. I'm a nobody."

Wrong. Each of us is a unique and special person created by God for special reasons. We may not have the gift of healing, or singing, or public speaking; but we do have special gifts. Maybe we have the ability to love the unloved, or to listen, or to say a kind word. Some of us may even have "handicaps" that the Lord plans to use for special reasons.

But remember, these gifts are given so we can serve others and help bring unbelievers into the kingdom. Let's pray that the Lord will reveal our gifts to each of us and His plan on how they'll be used.

Later, Jesus takes the disciples to a quiet place, probably for some rest. But the crowd finds them as usual. Instead of asking the crowd to leave, explaining that He and His disciples need some rest, Jesus actually welcomes the crowd, preaching and healing the sick. Even His time belongs to others.

The day is coming to an end, and the apostles are getting a little nervous. What are all these people going to eat? Here they are, out in the middle of nowhere, with 5,000 hungry men (not to mention all the women and children)!

Jesus' solution is simple: "You feed them."

"What! Are You kidding?" the disciples answer. "All we have is some kid's lunch—a little bread, a couple of fish. We can't do it."

Jesus patiently tells them how they *can* do it. The instructions sound crazy, but lately the disciples have been learning an important lesson: If God says to do it, do it—whether you understand it or not. They obey Jesus' command and shortly see over 5,000 full and satisfied people (plus 12 extra baskets of food).

Let Go

Once again we see Jesus praying.

And when He has finished, He turns to the apostles and asks them one of the most important questions they'll ever hear: "Who do you say that I am?" (9:20)

He's not asking for the popular answer. He zeros right in on what the apostles themselves believe. Jesus never sees crowds—only individuals. Each of us has to answer this question on his own.

Peter answers correctly, despite a popular Jewish view of Christ that's all wrong. Remember, the Jews are looking only at the prophecies that say He will come as a great political ruler. They ignore the prophecies that say He must suffer and die.

Because of this wrong idea, Jesus warns the apostles to tell no one who He is at this time, since some are already talking about starting a revolution and setting Him up as king.

He sets His disciples straight on exactly what is required of the Messiah (9:22). He must suffer, be rejected by the religious leaders, be killed, but raised up on the third day. (This isn't exactly the plan everyone has hoped for.)

In the verses that follow, we read about the fine print in our contract with God. It's one thing to give up our talents and abilities to serve Him and help others but quite another to be willing to give up our lives. Yet that's what He requires *if* we decide to follow Him.

The secret is to let go of our logical ways of winning wealth and glory.

Jesus continues by explaining the strange mystery of the Christian life—a mystery that has baffled mankind for centuries: Somehow, by giving up all that we have, or at least being willing to give it up, we receive life to the fullest. That defies our logic. Yet God promises that if we're willing to give up our lives, we live; if we're willing to give up our reputations, we're honored; if we're willing to give up money, we become wealthy; if we're willing to become last, we become first; if we're willing to become servants, we become great. Sounds strange—but God says it, and He has an interesting habit of always being right.

The Glory of God

No one today is sure what Jesus means when He says that there are some who won't taste death till they see the kingdom of God. There are a lot of different theories floating around. But perhaps the best explanation is the mountaintop experience that the three apostles are about to have.

Jesus takes Peter, John, and James with Him to the mountain to pray. It must be quite a long prayer because Peter and the other guys drop off to sleep. But Jesus keeps on praying. He's preparing to make a great exchange: His death for each of our lives, history's greatest event, and it's absolutely essential that He remain in perfect communion with the Father.

But as He continues to pray, a strange thing happens. His face begins to shine like the sun and His garments become as white as light (Matthew 17:2). For just a few moments, the apostles get to see Jesus in His heavenly glory.

There is only one description of Jesus in the entire New Testament. John describes the heavenly glory of Christ as it was revealed to him in a vision: Revelation 1:13-18. Stop right now and take a look at it.

Is this a picture of a weakling with sad eyes and a long face? This is Jesus as He is today in His full glory and power.

But there's more. They also see two Old Testament heroes talking with Jesus, discussing the great upcoming event of Jesus dying to buy His children back from Satan.

Peter is pretty shook up about the whole thing and starts babbling away about building tents and staying on the mountain—not really understanding what he's saying. However, it sounds as if he wants to keep this specific experience going as long as possible, forgetting about the people down below, forgetting about the sacrifice, and just focusing on himself and the other five up there.

But God has other plans. A cloud surrounds them and they hear, "This is My Son, My Chosen One; listen to Him!" (9:35)

Peter gets the point.

A Time of Weakness

Read Luke 9:37-62

Though there are a lot of events in this section, they all seem to point to the same problem—the weakness, the humanness of the people surrounding Jesus.

On the mountain, Jesus was surrounded by the power and glory of heaven. Now He suddenly finds Himself on earth, in the midst of struggling, unbelieving men. It's quite a comedown. Even His disciples seem to be experiencing a power shortage. They can't free a small boy from demon possession. Jesus is pretty disappointed in their unbelief, but He takes over and cures the boy.

While everyone is excited about the healing, Jesus again tries to explain to His disciples that He will have to make the ultimate sacrifice. But no one understands. Besides, there are more important matters to attend to, such as which one of the disciples might be the greatest!

They're probably careful not to let Jesus overhear this particular argument. (After all, He might get the wrong impression and think they're not humble.) But they've forgotten that God reads minds. Once again, Jesus reveals that mystery we've discussed. "He who is least among you, this is the one who is great" (9:48).

Later, John complains that other people are casting out demons in Jesus' name. Jesus tells him to leave the other people alone—they're all on the same team.

Still later, the Samaritans, who hate the Jews, give Jesus the cold shoulder. James and John, not quite understanding that their newfound powers are to be used in love, want to call down fire from heaven and destroy the people. Jesus sets them straight, of course.

Soon other people start coming to Jesus, wanting to follow Him. He makes it clear that there will be rough times for anyone who follows. He doesn't even have a place to call home. Others say they would like to follow Him, but they have a few things to do first.

Jesus makes it clear. Once we decide to go with Him, we go with Him. We don't look back.

Look—No Walls!

Day 5   *Read Luke 10:1-16*

Jesus calls a group of 70 followers together and asks them to pray that the Father will send more workers. More people would come to Jesus if they only knew the exact truth about Him—that He isn't a bunch of dusty, boring rules and regulations, that He's life at its fullest.

Jesus goes on to say that if the 70 let Him use them, they're like lambs in the middle of a pack of hungry wolves. Doesn't sound like the safest place to be, does it? But it is. Unlike others, they (or we) don't have to worry about putting up a plastic front, acting tough, or trying to act smooth and together. Those are just walls, barriers people build because they're afraid and want to protect themselves.

But they're already protected. They can be free from all those fears, free from having to build those walls. "In all things God works for the good of those who love Him" (Romans 8:28, NIV).

Jesus also teaches that if people listen to us when we're representing Him, they're listening to God. If people reject us because of Jesus, they're rejecting God.

Claim the Victory

The 70 are all excited about the authority Jesus has given them over Satan. Jesus says that nothing will injure them because through Him they now have authority over "all the power of the enemy" (10:19).

If we've given ourselves to Jesus, in His name we can have complete and total authority over Satan—in anything: bad habits, sin, thoughts, witnessing, sickness, demonic activity—*anything*.

But remember, Satan is a liar; and He'll use every lie in hell to make us think we haven't won, that nothing has changed, that we just can't have victory over that certain area in our lives. In fact, after we claim the victory, situations will often begin to appear worse. But it's all "appearance," a big front, a lie that Satan is using in a last desperate attempt to stop us.

Finally, Jesus praises the Father for choosing to reveal these truths to the childlike, those willing to admit they don't know everything, those who admit they need God.

The Journey, Not the Destination

The lawyer wants to know what he has to do to earn eternal life. Jesus answers with a parable: If we want to earn eternal life on our own, we have to love everybody as ourselves all the time. That's it. There's only one problem: None of us can do that.

As we study the tough requirements Jesus lays down, it's important to remember we can never meet them all the way. But complete obedience is exactly what the perfect God requires. Anything less, even just a little fudging, just won't cut it.

Jesus shows the impossibility of being perfect before God. He shows us our need to let Someone else take the punishment for our imperfections.

But there's more. Those requirements are also road signs that point toward our final goal of perfection. Jesus has even agreed to take us on that journey if we let Him. But remember, we'll never reach that final goal here on earth.

Jesus reminds Martha to keep her goal in mind and things in their proper perspective. In comparison to Jesus' teaching, how important is it whether we have lumpy gravy or not? We should remember what is eternal and what will last for only a short time.

A Few Tips on Prayer

Day 1   *Read Luke 11:1-13*

By now the disciples have seen the importance of prayer in Jesus' life. They ask Him to teach them how to pray. His example of prayer may seem a bit short to some of us, but it gets right to the point. Every word is important.

In the first line ("Father, hallowed be Thy name"), we see two key points. By using the word, "Father," Jesus once again points out that God the Father isn't a god who is way out there somewhere but the God who is concerned with every detail of our lives.

It's even good to thank God for things we aren't too crazy about.

"Hallowed be Thy name" shows the importance of praising God. Occasionally, we know we should pray, but just can't think of anything new to say. Or there are other times when we feel cut off from God, when we honestly don't feel a strong love for Him or feel His presence. It's good, especially on these occasions, just to sit back and begin thanking Him. It doesn't have to be for big things. It can be for the small, practically unnoticed blessings such as colors, smells, or textures. We can even begin thanking Him for things we're not too crazy about. Often, as a result of this praise, the love and joy once again begin growing inside us.

Look carefully at the rest of the prayer. In it, He teaches us to pray for His return, for our *daily* needs, for forgiveness (as we forgive others), and for keeping us from temptation.

Jesus explains that we must continue to ask, seek, and knock. Most of our fathers, as imperfect as they are, try to meet our needs and requests, even if their resources are limited. How much more will our perfect loving Father care for us and provide for our *every* need?

Gathering or Scattering?

After Jesus kicks out another demon, some people claim He's working for Satan. Jesus exposes the stupidness of this claim. How can Satan possibly hope to win at anything if he's fighting against himself? And what about other religious men? Are they casting out demons because they belong to Satan?

Jesus makes it clear that man has authority over Satan only because of the power of God. It's not our power that can crush Satan's stronghold, pierce his armor, and set people free. It's God's power, but He lets us use it.

Next, Jesus points out that it's impossible to remain neutral. If we're not helping Jesus gather people into His kingdom, then we're helping Satan scatter them.

The crowd keeps demanding a sign of His power, but Jesus refuses to perform tricks to satisfy their curiosity. In fact, He goes so far as to call them wicked. How easily others repented and listened to God in the past when mere men spoke. But today Someone far greater than a mortal man is standing before them!

He does, however, promise them the sign of Jonah. For three days and three nights Jonah was in the belly of a great fish and for three days and three nights people thought he was dead. But then the fish spit him out and once again Jonah was back with the living—a beautiful symbol of Jesus' coming death and resurrection.

But in order to benefit from His resurrection, we have to be open to Him. Jesus compares our eyes to lamps. The lamps let the Light into our bodies so we can see. But if our hearts are full of wrong thoughts, it makes the lenses of our lamps dirty. No Light can get in, and we're once again stumbling around in the dark. We should continually allow Jesus to wash our lenses so His light can shine in.

More Love

Sometimes it's hard to see that Jesus is acting in complete love, especially when He comes down as hard as He does on these people. But remember, total love also involves giving a person what he needs, not necessarily what he wants. There's more love in snatching a baby away from an oncoming train than in allowing him to play on the tracks. The same is true with the scribes and Pharisees. Jesus is simply trying to help them before it's too late to save them—it's all out of love.

Real love also means telling a person what he needs to hear.

The hand-washing here is not just to get clean hands. It's a complicated, man-made ritual. Jesus points out that His host should be just as concerned about cleaning his heart, since God also sees that.

Jesus calls the scribes and Pharisees "whitewashed tombs" (Matthew 23:27). On the outside they appear beautiful and clean. But on the inside they're full of death and decay.

People are the same today. They may go to church, give, smile, and go through all the outward actions. But if they don't allow Jesus to continually clean house, they're just as decayed inside as the bodies inside the tombs.

Jesus again calls the Pharisees tombs, this time "concealed tombs" (Luke 11:44). People are considered ceremonially unclean for a week if they so much as touch a tomb. Jesus says that they're just as dirty if they listen to the Pharisees. Pretty strong language.

A scribe complains that he is also being insulted and Jesus points out a few problems with scribes. Jesus says they're more concerned in following a religion, in setting up man-made rules and regulations, than in listening to the true Word of God. Consequently, they only love dead prophets (who can't condemn them). The scribes are just as anxious to kill living prophets as their fathers were.

Finally Jesus accuses the scribes of actually keeping people from knowing God. But instead of repenting, humbling themselves, and asking Jesus what they should do, the scribes and Pharisees begin plotting against Him.

More Truth

Day 4   *Read Luke 12:1-12*

Leaven is often used to symbolize sin. It can be either something like yeast, put into bread dough to make the dough go through a chemical change. Or it can be something like baking soda, used to create air holes in the dough and make it rise.

Jesus says that the leaven of the Pharisees (hypocrisy) will not be covered up forever. Hypocrisy is saying you're one thing and doing another—being a fake. A time will come when everything we hide, say, or do in secret will be "proclaimed on the housetops" (12:3). That could be a bit embarrassing unless, of course, we've already asked Jesus to forgive us.

He's even more concerned about us than we are about ourselves. Now that's caring!

Jesus again reminds us to keep things in their proper perspective. Don't fear man; he can only kill the body. Fear God; He's the One with all the power.

But He's also love. Jesus reminds us how loving and caring He is. If sparrows (less than ½¢ apiece at that time) are important to Him, how much more important are we, the ones He created in His own image? He's even more concerned about us than we are about ourselves. Now that's really caring!

Jesus teaches that blasphemy of the Holy Spirit will not be forgiven. But what is that? If someone scrapes his hand slightly, it will hurt. But if he scrapes it enough times, eventually a callous will form, and he won't feel as much pain. One of the Holy Spirit's ministries is to reveal Jesus and His truth. If the Holy Spirit is doing this for someone, but he continually refuses to accept the truth, eventually he'll no longer feel the Spirit's tug. He will have developed a spiritual callous. Then he's in real trouble.

Don't Worry!

A man complains that he isn't getting enough money from his brother. Jesus refuses to become part of a money squabble but explains how riches and possessions fit into a believer's life.

First, He warns us to guard against *every kind of greed* in our lives. Greed is a tricky thing. It can sneak into our lives and slowly begin controlling us till it eventually chokes out the love we should have for others. We become selfish and begin looking to see how we can advance our kingdom instead of God's.

Next, Jesus gives the parable of a man who only cares for himself, who chooses only to invest in the present. The trouble is, this life doesn't last forever. Jesus encourages us to invest in eternal things. Nobody will invest his life savings in a company he knows will soon go broke. Yet, today, that's exactly what many people are doing. Instead of investing in heaven (cooperating with God and helping others), they choose to invest in a life they know will end.

Unlike the rest of the world, Jesus says the believer does not have to rush around trying to make ends meet, trying to make enough money for food and clothes. God will provide these things.

When all our friends and the rest of the world are out there struggling to get things, it's difficult for us just to sit back and trust that God will provide everything we need. Yet that's what He promises. "And my God shall supply all your needs according to His riches in glory in Christ Jesus" (Philippians 4:19).

God will provide for us *if* we're doing what He asks. Let's not get caught up in the world's worries. "No soldier in active service entangles himself in the affairs of everyday life" (2 Timothy 2:4). If we've given ourselves to God, He's got our lives, our talents, *and* our worries. They're His now. Let's direct our energies toward resting in Him, and *doing His will*. Let Him take care of the rest.

Maybe Today

Jesus encourages us to be prepared for His return—to work as if He'll return today.

No one knows the exact time of Jesus' return. We can tell by various clues He's given us in Scripture that this is the general time, but no one knows the exact date—and for good reasons.

This way we have to stay on our toes. He knows us a lot better than we do. He knows the great temptation we have of putting things off till the last minute. If we knew Jesus was returning in five years instead of today, we'd lie back, maybe play a few of our old games with the world, and not even bother telling Uncle Harry about Jesus till the last minute. Unfortunately, our last minute may be a week after Harry's buried.

Jesus tells a parable about two stewards who have been given equal responsibilities. The first is busy working when the master arrives. The second figures he'll have plenty of time to get things right before the master returns. But the master returns unexpectedly and gives both stewards their reward: The first is put in charge of the master's possessions; the second is whipped—not so hot.

There's a good possibility that Jesus will come today. Let's be prepared in case He does.

Jesus Presses On

Fire often represents judgment in Scripture. Jesus is probably referring to the judgment of the world when He says He has "come to cast fire on the world" (12:49). How He wishes that His sacrifice isn't needed, that the judgment can begin now without it. But His love for us is too great. He has to be baptized with the agony, pain, and suffering of God's judgment for our sins through the sacrifice He knows is in His future.

He points out that many people can tell the weather by looking at the signs in the sky. Yet at the same time the same people refuse to look at the signs of the times. By calling them hypocrites, Jesus is pointing out that they could know the truth if only they wanted to.

Again Jesus points out that we're all guilty before God. There's no denying it. He encourages us through the parable of the magistrate to get our debts cleared with God before it's too late. We need to get our debts paid off by asking Jesus to forgive us, now, before He returns as the great Bill Collector.

Why Suffering?

Many people now listening to Jesus think that any sickness, suffering, or calamity is a judgment from God. They feel that anybody who has hardships and trials is simply being punished for his "unusually" wicked life. Jesus sets them straight. Pilate did not murder the Galileans because they were "greater sinners," nor did a tower fall on other people because they were exceptionally bad. Calamities are not always judgments from God. Often they are attacks from Satan.

If God can do anything, why does He sometimes do nothing?

If God is the God of love who can do anything, why does He sit back and do nothing when people suffer? And why do the more righteous sometimes get the worst of it? Can't God protect His own?

One answer can be found in the Book of James. "Consider it all joy, my brethren, when you encounter

88

various trials, knowing that the testing of your faith produces endurance. And let endurance have its perfect result, that you may be perfect and complete, lacking in nothing" (James 1:2-4).

God wants us to be "perfect and complete, lacking in nothing." Remember, we'll never see the total picture this side of heaven. We may not even know what He's perfecting in us, or what character qualities He's building. But we do know "God causes all things to work together for good to those who love God" (Romans 8:28).

God is the Coach. He wants to build our faith-muscles. Like a good Coach, He wants us to be able to perform at our best. Sometimes the workout is rough, but it's only to strengthen us. He promises never to take us beyond our endurance. "God is faithful; He will not let you be tempted beyond what you can bear" (1 Corinthians 10:13, NIV). Remember, He knows our limitations better than we do—trust Him.

Let's stop complaining and begin to look on the trials as God sees them: opportunities for us to grow, not terrible things for us to want to hurry up and get over with. Let's look on them as things for us to actually look forward to.

"Rejoice always . . . in *everything* give thanks" (1 Thessalonians 5:16, 18).

Really! Things Just Aren't Done That Way!

Day 2   *Read Luke 13:6-17*

Jesus tells another parable. A fig tree has been planted in a choice spot. Every year the owner comes looking for the fruit it's supposed to bear, and every year he finds nothing. For three years he does this.

Finally, when he feels there's no hope for the tree, he orders it to be cut down. "Why does it even use up the ground?" he asks. Yet he's persuaded to wait one more year. But if there's nothing after that year, it will come down for sure.

The same is true with God. He's putting off His return till that one last person receives Him. "The Lord is not slow about His promises, as some count slowness, but is patient toward you, not wishing for any to perish but for all to come to repentance. But the day of the Lord will come like a thief, in which the heavens will pass away with a roar and the elements will be destroyed with intense heat, and the earth and its works will be burned up" (2 Peter 3:9-10).

Though He is waiting, there will be a final judgment, a time when the Lord will say, "That's it. Cut them down. I've given them every chance."

Later, Jesus is teaching in a synagogue on the Sabbath when He sees a woman with a demon-inflicted sickness that causes her to stay bent over. Try walking around bent over for a couple minutes. Pretty painful? Now imagine doing that for 18 years!

Jesus heals her and she begins glorifying God.

But the synagogue official gets all flustered and complains that people shouldn't be healed on the Sabbath. Things just aren't done that way.

Jesus calls him (and a few others) a bunch of "hypocrites" (13:15). They will free their own animals on the Sabbath but not allow a fellow human to be healed.

Yet isn't the same true with us today? How many times do we do something a certain way because "that's the way it's done"? We feel a certain security in doing things the same way each time. But we don't need that false security. Things *can* be different. We have God.

Let Me Love You

The kingdom of God is more than just a "pie in the sky when we die." The "kingdom" is actually God's living presence in us and begins as soon as we receive the Lord. With Him comes His fruit: love, joy, peace, patience, kindness, goodness, faithfulness, gentleness, and self-control (Galatians 5:22-23).

Jesus compares the kingdom of God to the tiny mustard seed. Though it's extremely small, it will grow till it becomes a large tree. If we let Jesus grow in our lives, eventually we'll not only be able to stand firm and strong, but we'll actually reach out to others. But we have to allow Him to come inside and begin His work. We can't do it on our own.

Living in a Christian society, with Christian parents, Christian friends, even going to church, Sunday School, and youth group doesn't cut it.

When a man asks if only a few will be saved, Jesus compares heaven to a narrow door and says many won't make it. He refers to *Himself* in other passages as the Gate or Door. He's the only way to enter. "I am the Way, and the Truth, and the Life; no one comes to the Father, but through Me" (John 14:6).

The Door is wide open now. But someday it'll be sealed tight and no one will be able to get in. Many people will bang desperately on the Door and say they know Jesus. But His reply will be, "I don't know you; go away." Living in a Christian society, with Christian parents, Christian friends, even going to church, Sunday School, and youth group just won't cut it. The only way to heaven is through the Door, through Jesus.

Some Pharisees are concerned for Jesus' safety. They warn Him that Herod is out to kill Him. But Jesus will not run. The sacrifice, the substitution for our deaths, has to take place in Jerusalem; and that's where He's headed.

Finally, Jesus begins to mourn over Jerusalem. For centuries God has tried to reach out and embrace His children, but they turn Him down. How heartbreaking that must be when His own children refuse His love for them.

Be Humbled and Be Exalted

Day 4   *Read Luke 14:1-11*

A Pharisee invites Jesus to his house for a meal on the Sabbath. But this is no ordinary Pharisee. Most likely he's a member of the Sanhedrin—a group of the top religious men of the country.

It appears as if the host is setting Jesus up, for immediately a man appears with dropsy (a disease that causes a bloating of the body).

All are watching Jesus carefully to see what He will do. Will He heal the man on the Sabbath? Jesus asks for their opinions, but they refuse to answer. He heals the man, sends him on his way and zeros right in on the Pharisees. Which one of them would not pull his livestock out of a well on the Sabbath?

The question is so piercing and precise that the people can't answer, for once again, Jesus has revealed their true hearts (14:5-6).

Proud to be Humble

As He watches the invited guests scrambling for the most honored places at the dinner table, Jesus begins speaking about humility. We should take the lowest place, and if God wants to honor us, He will—but let's not do it ourselves.

As Scripture says, "God is opposed to the proud, but gives grace to the humble" (James 4:6).

94

What's the Motive?

Day 5   *Read Luke 14:12-14
and 1 Corinthians 13.*

Jesus turns to His host and tells him not to throw fancy banquets for those who can return the favor. Instead, the host should have feasts for the poor, the crippled, the lame, and the blind—those who can't repay.

How many times do we do something "loving" for someone with the wrong motive—hoping he'll return the favor, that someone will notice, or that somehow we'll get something in return?

There are several words for love in the Bible. Yet the greatest love is the love given by God, called *agape*. This is the love that gives without expecting anything in return, a love that says "you first," a totally unselfish love that would rather give than take. That's the love which motivated Jesus to die in our place. That's the love Jesus promises us. (Look at 1 Corinthians 13 for a deeper explanation of *agape*.)

Let's look for opportunities to exercise that love. Let's look for people we can help or perhaps invite home for dinner as Jesus commands. And what if they're "undesirable"? Praise God all the more. Remember, Jesus promises whatever we do to the *least* of His people, we're actually doing to Him. So treat that person as if he's Jesus—because in a sense he is.

What if we don't have that love right now? What do we do? Should we strain and struggle to manufacture it? Of course not. Like everything else, love has to come from God. We only receive it as we continue to let Him empty our old ways and replace them with Him.

Paul says, "If I have all faith, so as to remove mountains, but do not have love, I am nothing" (1 Corinthians 13:2).

UNLIKE WHAT THE WORLD SAYS, LOVE COMES <u>ONLY</u> FROM GOD.

Catch Me Later, God

As Jesus finishes talking about banquets, a man exclaims how fortunate everyone is who will be part of the great banquet in heaven. Naturally, the man figures he'll be included since he's "religious" and part of the chosen race. But Jesus begins a parable to make it clear that those who'll take part in His feast will not necessarily be the ones whom the man expects to see.

When a man gives a feast, he sends out invitations several days in advance. This is like what God did in the Old Testament. For centuries He was promising His chosen race that the Messiah would come. But when that day finally arrives, those He had originally invited refuse to believe His coming. Each one of them is too caught up in the world and its affairs to come and spend time with God.

Do the world's glitter and tinsel keep us from Jesus?

Is the same true with us? Do all of the world's glitter and tinsel keep us from Jesus? Do the worries, opportunities, work, friendships, and plastic pleasures of the world choke out our time with Jesus? Are we allowing Satan to dangle those distractions in front of us, hypnotizing us, convincing us to take our eyes off Jesus?

Let's continue to keep our eyes fixed on Him. Let's not refuse the invitation to dine and have fellowship with Him. Let's not let the noise of the world drown out the voice of God.

Jesus continues the parable. Since most of the religious leaders won't come to the feast, the slave is to invite the "sinners." But there aren't even enough then. Finally the host sends out invitations to the whole world.

And what about the men who were originally invited but refused? "For I tell you, none of those men who were invited shall taste of my dinner" (14:24).

The Cost

Jesus is on His way to the final showdown in Jerusalem. He knows what's coming and doesn't want the people to take their commitment to Him lightly. Perhaps here, more than anywhere else, He points out how much it costs to be His follower.

Jesus doesn't say we should hate our relatives (He's already said we should love everyone). He is saying, however, that our love for Him should be so intense, so full, that if He asks we should be willing to let go of the most precious, the most loved possessions or people in our lives.

What Jesus says about Christians carrying their own crosses has really become true. Thousands of Christians have died because they refused to deny Christ. Even today in Communist countries, many Christians are sitting in prison, being tortured, and dying because they will not deny Jesus.

Yet, are we willing to sound a little dumb to our unsaved friends by saying we're Christian or by standing up for what we believe around others?

There's still more to carrying the cross. We have to be willing to sacrifice our self-seeking interests so He can fill us with His plans (which, by the way, are far more interesting and fulfilling).

To follow Him, we have to *be willing to let Him help us give up everything*. That's not to say we have to sell everything and live in the street, but when it comes down to a choice between something or someone and Jesus—it has to be Jesus.

Jesus says we're to be salt. Salt is used for two things: to keep food from decaying and to bring out its flavor. If we're salty salt (filled with Jesus' power), we can help stop the world from decaying—or at least slow down the rotting. If we're close to Jesus, even our presence will often stop the people from acting quite so bad.

And like salty salt, we can bring out the true flavor of life: its joys and its real pleasures not only for our lives but for the lives of people around us.

Yet, if we're unsalty salt, we have no power to preserve the world or to bring taste to others' lives.

But praise God, for He can restore all things, even our saltiness, if we ask Him.

When Angels Throw Parties

Day 1   *Read Luke 15:1-10*

The Pharisees have strict religious rules warning them never to associate with "sinners" (people who do not follow their tough religious regulations). Not only does Jesus spend time with the "sinners," He goes so far as to eat some meals with them.

The Pharisees and scribes are outraged and grumble among themselves. Once again, it's time for them to learn an important truth about God; so Jesus begins the parable of the lost sheep.

When one sheep is lost, a good shepherd will leave the others and hunt all night for the one helpless, lonely sheep. Bruised, battered, and scratched from the rough terrain, the shepherd will not quit till he has found that sheep. And when he finds it he doesn't whip or scold it, but joyfully picks it up and carries it all the way back to the flock.

None of the world's man-made religions speak of the God who actually searches for His "children." Many people think that if we come crawling to God or fight and struggle our way up to Him, He'll eventually receive us. But Jesus speaks of the God who actually goes out to us.

"Behold, I Myself will search for My sheep and seek them out" (Ezekiel 34:11).

"I will seek the lost, bring back the scattered, bind up the broken, and strengthen the sick" (34:16).

"I will feed them in a good pasture, and their grazing ground will be on the mountain heights" (34:14). That's some God!

That's some God!

The next parable, about the woman and the lost coin, goes into even more detail about the effort the Lord puts out to find each of His lost ones. His Lamp is the Holy Spirit, and He continually shines into the darkness of men's hearts, revealing the truth and calling them home.

What happens when someone finally lets God the Son pick him up and carry him home? Well, the angels throw a party.

"Welcome Home"

Day 2   *Read Luke 15:11-24*

This is the last of three parables Jesus gives to the scribes and Pharisees to clear up their wrong ideas of what God is like.

Like so many of us, the younger son demands to do things his way. He wants all of the wealth his father will give him so he can spend it on himself and have a good time.

The father, knowing his son will not listen to him, finally agrees. So many times God will try to warn us to stay away from certain things. But so many times we'll refuse to listen. Eventually, knowing it's the only way we'll learn, He lets us have our way. He tells us about the brick walls, but we'll often refuse to listen and end up running into them head-on.

This is what happens to the son. Suddenly he finds himself working for a stranger in a foreign land. He also gets the privilege of working with pigs, walking around in raw garbage and sewage, feeding them. It's not quite like the "good times" he had planned. He's so hungry that even the pigs' food looks good to him.

He knew he had to return to his father when "he came to his senses" (15:17). Jesus says we're really not ourselves till we realize our need to come back to Him.

The son has it all planned. He'll admit his sins, ask for forgiveness, and force himself to suffer for his selfishness by becoming one of his father's servants.

But apparently the father has been anxiously waiting for his son's return, because he sees him from "a long way off" (15:20). Instead of scolding or agreeing that maybe the son should suffer a little for his selfishness, the father rushes to him, hugs and kisses him (garbage-coated clothes and all), gives him a robe (a symbol of high position), a ring (symbol of authority), and plans a great feast in his honor.

That's how loving our Father is, anxiously waiting for each of His children to "come to his senses" and come home so He can embrace him and direct all of His overflowing love and boundless joy toward him.

Infinite Is Infinite

Day 3   *Read Luke 15:25-32*

Jesus finishes the parable. As we say, the youngest son represents the "sinners," those who have strayed away from God. But the oldest son, the one who comes in from the field, represents the scribes and Pharisees, the ones caught up in "churchianity." They're the ones who have been serving their Father long and diligently.

We see that the oldest son is so angry he won't go in and share his father's and brother's great joy (15:28).

Even though his father actually begs him, he still refuses. The reason? "For so many years I have been serving you, and I have never neglected a command of yours; . . . but when this son of yours came, who has devoured your wealth . . ., you kill the fattened calf for him" (15:29-30).

But in his argument the older brother reveals the real problem. By his words we see that he has always considered his relationship with his father more like that of a servant to a master than of a father to a son. On the surface, it appears that he has stayed closest to his father; but in his heart he has strayed even farther than his brother. He's completely forgotten the free, spontaneous love that should exist between a father and child. He now serves his father almost grudgingly.

But out of love the father tries to explain to the oldest that he's always had free access to anything he wanted, including the father's love. The son chose to make their relationship slavish bondage when there was no need. A share of the father's possessions and all his love have always been his. It was only in pride that the oldest son felt he had to earn it.

God's love is infinite. Infinite is infinite. He doesn't love one person infinitely more than another.

For the scribes and Pharisees, this parable drives the truth of God's unconditional love even deeper. God's love for man is infinite. If we sin, he loves us infinitely. We may make Him sad, but He loves us infinitely. If we are righteous, He loves us infinitely. Infinite is infinite; He doesn't love one person more infinitely than another.

Riches

This parable is considered to be one of the more difficult ones to understand. A steward, who has been put in charge of a rich man's estate, is squandering the riches. His boss hears about it and threatens to fire him. But before the threat can be carried out, the steward, knowing he has no skills to support himself, puts a shrewd plan into action.

He begins treating all of his boss' debtors with great kindness, hoping they'll return the favor and allow him to live in one of their homes when he's kicked out of his. One man owes 900 gallons of olive oil; the steward changes it to 450. Another owes 1,200 bushels of wheat, he reduces it to 960.

Like the steward, the people of the world are very clever, sometimes more so than Christians. If only Christians would be as hardworking and diligent to spread the Good News as they are to get riches and comfort. Jesus tells us to use what wealth we have to help others (16:9).

Who's Controlling Whom?

Jesus promises us freedom from whatever worldly thing controls us. If we haven't asked for that freedom, we're all under some sort of bondage. In a real sense, we're all slaves to something: the desire for riches, or fame, or power, or popularity, or drugs, or sex, or security, or greatness—something. If Jesus hasn't stepped in, we're all under the world's bondage in one way or another.

Sometimes the freedom we get from our faith in Jesus doesn't come all at once. Sometimes it's two steps forward and a stumble, two steps more and another stumble. But eventually, we will be free if we really want to be.

But what if we don't? What if we want to follow Jesus yet continually let ourselves be controlled by something else? Jesus says either we'll wind up loving Him and hating the worldly master or hating Him and loving the worldly master.

So if we love Jesus, let's continue to love Him. He'll take care of the other master *if* we let Him and cause us to hate it to the point of wanting to be free of it.

Jesus says that we cannot serve both God and anything else. That's not to say that money and other things people think "desirable" are wrong. But rather, "the *love* of money is a root of all sorts of evil" (1 Timothy 6:10). The Lord often uses money to accomplish His purposes. There's nothing inherently wrong with wealth itself. But we have to make sure we're controlling the wealth instead of having it control us.

The Pharisees make fun of Jesus. They think a person's wealth is an indication of how good that person is. As a result, they have quite a lust for money.

But Jesus shakes them up. Though they may be putting on a show of holiness for the people, God knows their hearts. He goes on to say that the very thing they love, "that which is highly esteemed among men is detestable in the sight of God" (16:15).

SOMETIMES LIFE IS
TWO STEPS AND A STUMBLE.
IT WAS FOR FIRST-
CENTURY CHRISTIANS TOO.

Settle Only for the Best

John the Baptist's ministry marked the end of an age, an age lasting 4,000 years, during which God was revealed through the Law (Ten Commandments, etc.) and the prophets. Now Jesus begins a new age where the Holy Spirit lives inside of us, revealing and directing.

Yet the Law is still holy and will never change. "But *if you are led by the Spirit,* you are not under the Law" (Galatians 5:18).

This doesn't mean we should go out and begin doing anything we please. *If we're led by the Spirit,* we begin doing the right things (or not doing them) not because we think we have to, but because we want to. There's a big difference.

> *God loves us so much that He wants us to have the very best—not some second- or third-rate counterfeit.*

Jesus illustrates this point by speaking against adultery (sex outside marriage). In other places the Bible teaches that fornication (sex before marriage) is also wrong.

But why? In this day and age when many are doing it, why can't we go all the way or live with somebody?

God loves us so much that He wants us to have the very best—not some second- or third-rate counterfeit. Sex was created as the supreme expression of love between a husband and wife. Through the years, marriage partners continue to grow and become one both emotionally and spiritually (just as we are becoming one with Jesus) and sex grows and blossoms as a result of that oneness. Love is supposed to be the supreme expression physically of what's happening to a couple emotionally and spiritually.

But Satan has taken that beauty and tried to counterfeit it with the popular idea: "Give it to me now, I've got to have it."

Unfortunately, if we've experienced Satan's type of sex, it's often more difficult to have a complete relationship with our future partner. There will be deep emotional scars that will make it very difficult to let down all of our defenses and become truly one with our future husband or wife.

The Sin of Uncaring

For the time being, this is Jesus' final teaching on the dangers of being rich. In it we see a rich man dressed in the best clothes and living it up every day.

When he dies, he finds himself in hell. But why? He didn't do anything. Unfortunately, that's the problem. Though he saw poor old Lazarus starving and full of sores outside his gates, he refused to help. He refused to acknowledge the responsibilities of being rich.

Again, there's nothing inherently wrong with being rich; but it does mean we have far greater responsibilities. We must continually allow the Spirit to remind us whose money it really is and find out exactly what He wants done with it.

Money tends to make us feel independent, to feel we don't need God quite as much as we used to. "After all, if God fails me I still have my bank account." But the Bible says:

Give me neither poverty nor riches;
Feed me with the food that is my portion,
Lest I be full and deny Thee and say,
    "Who is the Lord?"
Or lest I be in want and steal,
And profane the name of my God (Proverbs
    30:8-9).

Back to the rich man. Even though he's in hell, he still feels he's superior to Lazarus and actually asks him to bring water and to warn his brothers.

But Abraham points out that the brothers need no more warnings. The entire Old Testament points to Jesus. Besides, if they won't listen to Scripture, there's no way they'll listen to someone raised from the dead. Miracles seem to make little difference when people don't want to believe. Including Himself, Jesus raised four people from the dead; yet today people will find any excuse they can to deny this fact so they can continue running their own lives.

WEEK 9

Faith

Day 1   *Read Luke 17:1-6*

Jesus tells His disciples that Christians will stumble in their daily lives. This, Jesus says, is unavoidable. But how terrible it will be for those who cause the stumbling. It would be better for them to suffer a terrible death than to cause someone else to sin.

Next, Jesus warns us to encourage one another to clean up our acts. "If your brother sins, rebuke him" (17:3). Any "rebuking" should be done in love and understanding to a person's face (not behind his back).

Later the apostles think they need more faith and ask for it. But the problem isn't that they need more faith. They need the right kind of faith—God's faith.

God's faith is a definite, absolute assurance, a quiet knowing that He can do anything. This faith is so powerful that if we only have a mustard seed's worth we can move trees or mountains.

Where can we get this brand of high-powered faith? A lasting faith comes from God. "Jesus [is] the Author and Perfector of faith" (Hebrews 12:2).

And how do we get it? "Faith comes from hearing, and hearing by the Word of Christ" (Romans 10:17).

More Healing

After we receive Jesus Christ and begin working for Him, it is often difficult to remain humble. We begin to think we deserve special privileges for all the good things we've done. But remember, there's nothing we did to earn God's love. For instance, the lepers Jesus heals have done nothing to deserve His special attention. As His servants, it's a privilege to serve Him.

As Jesus continues on His way to Jerusalem, He enters a town and meets 10 lepers. Because of the laws concerning their disease, the lepers must remain at a distance from Him. But they call out to Him, asking for mercy.

Without any fancy hocus-pocus, Jesus simply tells them to show themselves to the priest, who would make a public statement that they were clean. Jesus doesn't need to be loud; He doesn't have to work a person or crowd into wild-eyed excitement. The Lord simply speaks, and it's done—just as He spoke in the beginning when He created the universe.

But only one of the 10 returns to thank Him (and a Samaritan at that!) Jesus is saddened over the lack of gratitude from the others but promises that the one man will be saved. Let's take the time to thank God for what He has given us in our lives.

As in the Days of Noah

The Pharisees have heard Jesus speak of the kingdom of God before. This time they ask Him when it will come into being. Jesus' explanation has two meanings; in both cases He points out that the kingdom is already here!

Jesus first explains that He, who is God and contains everything God is (including the kingdom), is in their midst. Second, Jesus explains that the kingdom of God begins in a believer's heart. If we receive Jesus, the kingdom begins as a tiny seed planted inside us. As we continue to let the Holy Spirit control our lives, the kingdom begins to grow and eventually produces fruit.

Jesus explains that His second coming will be like a brilliant bolt of lightning. People will no longer have a chance to repent. Christians will be taken away from non-Christians. God is holding off on His coming, not wishing for any to perish. But when He returns, people won't have time to change their minds.

Just as in Noah's day, when Christ returns, people will be involved in their selfish day-to-day affairs. And we, like Noah, have been given God's Word and are to tell people that He'll once again return to judge us.

Jesus explains that those who are still decaying spiritually will be devoured by God's judgment, as vultures tear at decaying flesh.

More on Prayer

Day 4   *Read Luke 18:1-8*

We live in an instant society: instant potatoes, instant breakfast, even instant money. In this generation, more than in any other, people often become frustrated and discouraged if they don't get an immediate response to their prayers. In this section, Jesus gives a parable to show we should not give up.

In this parable we are represented by the helpless widow who must rely on the judge for protection. She persists in asking the judge for justice; and eventually the judge, even though he has no respect for God or man, gives in just to shut her up. If the judge, as evil and unloving as he is, will grant justice, how much more will our perfect and loving Father answer our prayers for justice?

God answers prayer in three ways:

"Yes."

"No—that's second best; I want you to have the best."

"Yes, but wait."

Often it's this last answer that's the most difficult to accept. As the days, weeks, months, even years go by, we begin to get discouraged. We begin to doubt that God really hears. Nothing could be further from the truth.

More on Humility

Few things cause as much trouble for the Christian as pride. We often become puffed up with pride, thinking we're better than the next guy for some stupid reason or other. But that's a lie. We're all equally guilty before God—and equally forgiven.

No one is perfect. No one. "If we say that we have no sin, we are deceiving ourselves; and the Truth is not in us" (1 John 1:8). The only reason we can step into God's presence is because Jesus has taken the rap for all of our sins. We've done nothing fantastic but receive a gift that's available to anyone.

Yet how many times do we judge someone who commits obvious sins when we have some that are just as bad? The only difference is that ours are hidden a little better.

Yes, we are to encourage one another, to try to become purer—but in love, not out of self-righteousness or pride. We are also to "confess [our] sins to one another" (James 5:16). That should cure us of most of our self-inflation.

Finally, Jesus points out that we should trust Him as a child trusts his father.

Jesus = God

A rich ruler who has led a pretty good life still feels something is lacking and wants to know how to receive eternal life. Jesus sees that, though the man may be sincere, he still has another god—riches. In order to let God be Lord, Jesus tells the man to give up his other god and follow Him.

This saddens the ruler. Jesus explains how difficult it is for the rich to enter the kingdom of God. Riches aren't bad, but with them it's often difficult to let Jesus be first.

Jesus Is God

Many people use 18:18-19 as proof that Jesus isn't God. But that's not the case at all. Jesus wants the ruler to reflect on his own words when he calls Jesus "good Teacher." If no one is good except God, and the ruler calls Jesus good, he's actually calling Jesus "God."

Jesus' deity is shown throughout the New Testament. As He approaches the end of His mission on earth, He prays that He might once again share the same glory with the Father He had before the world was created (John 17:5).

In John 10:30, we read still another claim that Jesus makes of Himself: "I and the Father are one."

In John 1:1-3, we see that Jesus created "all things" and was "with God" and "was God."

In Colossians 1:16, we see again that Jesus created all things.

And yet with all of that power, all of that glory, He is still willing to die for us so we can spend eternity with Him. "Christ Jesus, who, though He existed in the form of God, did not regard equality with God a thing to be grasped, but emptied Himself, taking the form of a bond servant, and being made in the likeness of men. . . . He humble[s] Himself by becoming obedient to the point of death, even death on a cross" (Philippians 2:5-8).

Preparing the Twelve

Day 7   *Read Luke 18:28-43*

Jesus has just mentioned how difficult it is for the rich to enter the kingdom of God when Peter, who sounds a little nervous, begins justifying himself. Jesus consoles him by saying anyone who has sacrificed for the kingdom will be rewarded both in heaven and on earth.

Next, Jesus takes His twelve aside and explains that they're about to complete their trip to Jerusalem and "all things which are written [in the Old Testament] about the Son of Man will be accomplished" (18:31). He has told them about this before, but now He gets to the details. "For He will be delivered up to the Gentiles, and will be mocked and mistreated and spit on; and after they have scourged Him, they will kill Him; and the third day He will rise again" (18:32-33).

Yet the apostles still don't get the point. They are still looking forward to some great political kingdom.

Later, as they approach Jericho, a blind man cries out to Jesus for mercy. He's not proud or self-conscious. He needs Jesus, and he calls out to Him for help—refusing to be intimidated by what others may say or think. Jesus stops and heals him on the spot. His faith has made him well.

WEEK 10

A Little Guy with an Empty Heart

Day 1   *Read Luke 19:1-10*

Jericho is on the main highway, 17 miles northeast of Jerusalem. So all the trade that comes from the East must pass through it. Tax collectors have a field day collecting outrageous custom taxes from the weary but wealthy merchants. And there are many such collectors hanging around, hoping to cash in on the spoils. Zaccheus is one of the more successful ones.

Yet he feels a need for something more than piles of money. He's too short, so he rushes ahead of the crowd and climbs a tree to get a better view of Jesus.

Zaccheus is a man who has to keep up his tough-guy image, but he's willing to look like a fool. He's willing to scamper up a tree and forget some of his precious pride *so he can see Jesus.*

And the Lord honors Zaccheus' humility. He stops, calls Zaccheus by name, and invites Himself home for the evening. Zach is pretty excited and jumps down to join Him.

Once again, the self-righteous people grumble because Jesus is associating with such a man. But the Lord knows that Zaccheus truly wants something to fill the spiritual emptiness he knows that he has in his heart.

We don't read of Jesus saying another word, but suddenly Zach offers to give half of what he has to the poor and to repent and to give back four times as much as he has "stolen." It's interesting that Jesus' very presence can touch and change lives.

Much Is Given — then Much Is Required

As Jesus approaches Jerusalem, people still think He will set up a political kingdom as soon as He arrives. To straighten out their wrong idea, He begins another parable.

In the parable, Christ is represented by the nobleman who goes to a distant country to receive a kingdom. But, like the ruler, Jesus will come back.

Till He returns, He has given each of us certain talents, gifts, and riches to use for Him. Some of us will use His gifts well and let Him accomplish much through us, while others will be less dedicated.

But there are yet others who are afraid to use their God-given talents because they may misuse or become proud of them. How sad. Let's not forget "there is no good tree which produces bad fruit" (6:43). If we love the Lord and want to serve Him, let's trust Him. Let's trust that He'll direct our gifts as we step out to use them for Him.

What about the folks who refuse to submit to the Nobleman, who refuse to let Him be Lord? Jesus is pretty specific. "But these enemies of Mine, who did not want Me to reign over them, bring them here, and slay them in My presence" (19:27).

The Stones Will Cry Out!

Day 3   *Read Luke 19:28-40*

After thousands of years, the event mankind has been waiting for so anxiously finally takes place. The Messiah enters His holy city. This event had been predicted by the prophet Zechariah over 500 years before, and now it is coming true exactly as he has prophesied!

Behold, your King is coming to you;

He is just and endowed with salvation,

Humble, and mounted on a donkey (Zechariah 9:9).

The Pharisees try to silence the crowd as Jesus rides into the city on a donkey colt, but He explains that if they became silent the very stones would cry out!

What does He mean? Granted, sometimes the elements seem to worship God by their very beauty and splendor (often more than we do), but Jesus is referring to something supernatural—the stones would literally cry out!

About 607 B.C. the angel Gabriel visited Daniel and explained in symbolic terms that the Messiah would arrive 483 prophetic years from the time the decree went out to rebuild Jerusalem in 445 B.C. (Daniel 9:24). And it is this year to the exact day that Jesus arrives in Jerusalem! No wonder He chooses this day to finally allow the people to hail Him as Messiah.

The time is finally right.

The Entrance

Day 4   *Read Luke 19:41-48*

In the middle of the celebration of Jesus' arrival in Jerusalem (19:37), He begins to weep. Perhaps "weep" isn't the best word, for the original Greek text says He is full of agony and sobbing violently over the people of Jerusalem.

If only they would accept Him as God the Son. If only they would realize this is the day they have been waiting for. If only they would stop trying to run their own lives and let God be Lord. Then they would have the peace they so desperately need.

But they won't accept Him, and Jesus knows the terrible consequences. Because they refuse to recognize the time of God's "visitation," the entire city will be leveled by its enemies. In A.D. 70, less than 40 years after Jesus makes this prediction, the Roman army will completely demolish Jerusalem.

Since this is the time of the Passover celebration, Jews are coming to Jerusalem from all over to celebrate and make sacrifices at the temple. Since only Jewish money can be used in the temple, the money-changers are making outrageous profits by changing foreign currency into Jewish money at sky-high exchange rates. Likewise, those wishing to make sacrifices usually have to buy animals at the temple (at a ridiculous price), since the officials will usually find the animals the people bring to be "unfit for sacrifice."

The people are actually being exploited and robbed

as they try to worship God. This is what Jesus is reacting to so strongly when He flings the tables over and chases the money-changers away.

Imagine how angry the priests and scribes are. Here is the Man they are trying to kill, preaching openly inside their temple; and there's absolutely nothing they can do about it—there'd be a riot if they would arrest Jesus now. But the priests and scribes keep waiting. They know there will be a time that's right.

A Trick Question

Jesus continues teaching in the temple, the stronghold of the people who are trying to have Him killed. Yet the temple was built as a place to worship God.

The chief priests, scribes, and elders demand to know who gave Jesus the authority to teach, heal, and act so boldly. They're not nearly as concerned about the truth as they are about trying to trip up Jesus. If Jesus slips just once, they can arrest Him for breaking one of the thousands of Jewish or Roman laws.

Jesus, knowing they are already aware of His claims as Messiah, throws the question back to them. "Was the baptism of John from heaven or from man?"

What a dilemma. If they admit that the baptism was from God, then they'd have to accept John's claims that Jesus is the Messiah. Even though John has baptized thousands of them, they pretend they don't know. Jesus, knowing they know, refuses to tell them where His authority comes from.

Instead, He begins a parable: God has planted a vineyard (Israel) and put His chosen people (the Jews and religious officials) in charge of it. Through the years, He has sent several prophets to the people, asking them to receive His message (His proper place in their lives). But they refuse the prophets and beat them. Still, God in His patience continues sending more prophets and still the people refuse to listen to them. Finally He sends His Son, but the people kill Him.

As a result, God promises to destroy the unfaithful vine growers and give the vineyard to others.

Those listening cannot believe that such a thing will happen, but Jesus explains that anyone who rejects Him will likewise be rejected by the Father.

Another Trick Question

Day 6   *Read Luke 20:19-26*

The religious officials continue to keep a close eye on Jesus. They've been humiliated by the parable of the vine grower and have been exposed to the crowd for what they really are. So they begin a new plan of attack—sending men who pretend they are seriously seeking truth, to try to tie Jesus up in His own words.

The men ask their first question and try to disguise its dangers with a lot of flattery. But how can the question, "Is it lawful for us to pay taxes to Caesar?" be so dangerous?

Remember, the Israelites have two rulers: their religious leaders and the Roman government. The deeply religious feel that only God is their King, and to pay tribute to any other authority is a terrible act of idolatry. If Jesus says, "Pay Caesar," He will alienate many sincere and God-loving people. On the other hand, if He says, "Don't pay," He will be arrested by the Roman government. It looks as if the questioners have Him cornered.

But Jesus turns around and answers them with wisdom. Money with Caesar's face stamped on it is Roman money. If the Romans want it, let them have it. But your body, mind, and soul belong to God.

That's quite an answer. It's so precise that the men who are trying to trick Jesus are left speechless.

And Still Another

The Sadducees, who do not believe in the resurrection (life after death), try to make Jesus look ridiculous and prove Him wrong with a ridiculous question. According to the Law, if a man dies without a child to carry on the family name, his brother must marry the widow and produce a child. Now if this happens seven times, and there is a resurrection as Jesus says, then to whom will she be married in heaven?

Jesus points out that their entire argument is based on a wrong assumption. The Sadducees' error is in thinking that life carries on in heaven as it does on earth.

Life after death is a fact, not something to waste time arguing about.

Jesus continues to point out that resurrection is a fact, not something to waste time arguing about. When describing Himself to Moses, God explained that He is still the God of Abraham, Isaac, and Jacob—meaning that they are still living (Leviticus 26:42). We see that Jesus' answer is so impressive that no one has the "courage to question Him any longer about anything" (Luke 20:40).

But the people have many more wrong ideas, and

Jesus tries to correct them. The people know from prophecies that the Messiah is a descendant of David, and they are correct. (Joseph was from the line of David.) Jesus is also David's Lord.

Finally, Jesus warns the people about the scribes, men who say they love God but are much more concerned about building their own kingdoms than working to build God's.

Sounds a little like people today, doesn't it?

WEEK 11

"By Your Perseverance You Will Win"

Day 1   *Read Luke 21:1-24*

The rich noisily drop their large offerings into the collection box while a poor widow puts in all she has, two lepta (a small coin worth about one-eighth of a cent). Jesus notices and points out that she has contributed more than all of the other people combined. She's given all she has, not because she feels an obligation, but because she trusts that the Lord will provide for her needs.

Someone points out the splendor of the temple and Jesus prophesies that everything they see will be torn down. Everything. The temple is used to worship God. But if the people refuse God, what good is it? It becomes nothing but a worthless shell, another empty ritual for "churchianity."

The men ask for signs as to when this destruction will take place. Instead of a definite date, Jesus gives them events that will lead up to it. Though He's referring to the destruction of Jerusalem in A.D. 70, keep in mind that, according to the Book of Revelation, many of the same events will also happen before His second coming.

Jesus warns that many will say they are Christians

or even that they are the Messiah. He goes on to say that there will be many wars, famines, plagues, even signs from heaven; but we are still not to worry.

And before all that, many Christians will be beaten, murdered, and dragged into court. This persecution is happening in some countries even today. But we shouldn't be afraid. We still have many opportunities to share Jesus with an unsaved world. We shouldn't plan what to say; He'll provide the words. "I will give you utterance and wisdom which none of your opponents will be able to resist or refute" (21:15). He tells His followers, "You will be hated by all on account of My name" (21:17), even by relatives and friends. We should just hang in there and we'll win.

Run to the Mountains

Jesus tells the people that when an army surrounds Jerusalem, they are to flee to the mountains. When the Roman army approached Jerusalem in A.D. 67, the Christians who did just that were saved. But those who trusted in their own strength instead of God's Word suffered the consequences. According to Josephus, a historian living at that time, 1,100,000 people were murdered and 97,000 were taken prisoner.

What a needless waste. Yet how many times do we ignore God and choose to do things our way, only to run into problems eventually.

Be On Guard—Pray

Day 2   *Read Luke 21:25-38*

In the last verse of yesterday's reading, we learned that eventually Gentiles will no longer trample Jerusalem. For centuries men scoffed at this prediction; but in 1948, to the world's surprise, Israel became a nation. For the first time since A.D. 70, Israel once again belonged to the Jews. In 1967 they surprised the world again by reclaiming the entire city of Jerusalem.

The world is coming under new management.

Jesus mentions other events that will take place shortly before His return. There will be signs in the sun, moon, and stars. The nations will be dismayed; many will be perplexed at the roaring of the sea. Men will actually begin to faint from fear. In the Book of Revelation, plagues, famines, and earthquakes (just to name a few disasters) are mentioned as parts of God's plan. But this should come as no surprise to us. After all, the world is coming under new management; and God is cleaning up His place before He comes to take charge.

When others may be fainting from fear, Jesus tells us to raise our heads in anticipation, for He will be coming "in a cloud with power and great glory" (21:27). When a tree begins to bud, we know that spring is here. Likewise, when we see certain things happening, we should realize that Jesus is about to pay us His final visit.

Verse 32 ("This generation will not pass away till all things take place") has caused problems for some people. Some scholars point out that the Greek word used for "generation" can also mean "a race" or "a people." It's possible Jesus means the Jewish race will not pass away till Jesus' prophecies have been fulfilled. Other scholars say the word "generation" should be interpreted literally—that Christ is referring to the destruction of Jerusalem as a symbol of His second coming.

More importantly, Jesus says that His words will never pass away, regardless of what happens to the rest of the universe.

Jesus also warns us to be on guard and not get tangled up in the world's artificial pleasures or worries, for when He comes, His judgment will come as unexpectedly as a trap slams shut.

And what are we to do? "Keep on the alert at all times, *praying* in order that [we] may have strength to escape all these things that are about to take place, and to stand before the Son of Man" (21:36).

Some Heavy-Duty Symbolism

Day 3   *Read Luke 22:1-13*
                         and Exodus 12:1-13

Passover always draws a large crowd to Jerusalem, and the priests and scribes are afraid they might start a riot if they try to arrest Jesus in front of everyone. Still, something has to be done; after all He's actually trying to *teach* the people Himself. Besides, He just doesn't fit into their mold. Judas solves their dilemma when he sells out to Satan. He tells the officials when Jesus will be free from the crowds so they can arrest Him in secret.

Later, the day before Passover, Jesus instructs Peter and John to prepare the meal for that evening. Let's look at Passover for a moment. (Take a couple minutes to read Exodus 12:1-13.) On the first Passover the Jews were not only freed from being Egyptian slaves but were also spared God's judgment on Egypt—on the condition that they act in faith and do as He commands.

But there's another side to this Passover story. The Jews were to sacrifice a one-year-old, perfect male lamb. Dozens of times in Scripture Jesus, who is perfect and without sin, is referred to as the Lamb.

The people could only cook the lamb by roasting it completely in fire. Remember, fire symbolizes judgment; and Jesus will feel the complete judgment of God that otherwise would fall on us.

Through Jesus we are not only freed from our bondage to sin but are also spared God's judgment on the world—if we act in faith and receive Jesus as He asks.

The Jews in Egypt could only be saved by putting the lamb's blood around the doorways of their homes. We can only be saved by the blood of Jesus—His death on the cross.

And, just so no one misses the connection, God chooses to sacrifice His Son on exactly the same day as the original Passover! (If you want to figure this out for yourself, don't forget that the new Jewish day begins at sunset, not midnight.)

Last Passover, First Communion

Day 4   *Read Luke 22:14-30*

The meal is finally ready. Jesus explains how He has been longing to celebrate this particular Passover with them and that the ultimate sacrifice will begin shortly.

He picks up some unleavened bread and breaks it, explaining that this represents His body which He is giving to them (and to us). His pure, sin-free body will go through extreme agony for us. The next time we share communion, let's keep that in mind.

Next, Jesus picks up a cup of wine, saying that it represents His blood which will shortly be poured out from His body for them.

His death will make a new agreement between man and God—His death is traded for ours. Only the sacrifice of God Himself is strong enough to pay for our sins.

God is the God of love and also the God of justice. Legally, we should pay for our sins. But God loves us so much He doesn't want to see us suffer. Still, because He's a God of justice, somebody must pay. The solution? He'll pay for our sins Himself. He'll suffer. He'll endure the pain that should be ours.

That's Some Love!

Again, Jesus mentions that someone in the group will betray Him. At first the disciples show concern, but soon the concern turns into a debate as to which of them is the greatest disciple.

Once again Jesus points out that the greatest follower is the one whose life is most like that of a servant. At one point, Jesus kneels down and actually washes each disciple's feet (John 13:5). Imagine, God washing our feet! But that's where greatness lies—in serving.

Finally, Jesus promises them the privilege of eating at His heavenly table and the opportunity to actually rule along with Him.

Separating the Chaff

Day 5   *Read Luke 22:31-38*

Previously, Jesus changed Simon's name to Peter ("Rock"). But now He calls him Simon again as if to remind Peter of his old self, his old human weaknesses.

Satan has gotten permission from God to test Peter, to see if he will give in to his weaknesses. Satan hopes that Peter's determination to serve the Lord will blow away like chaff.

Chaff is the outside husk surrounding the wheat kernel, a part of the stalk that can't be eaten. To separate the chaff from the wheat, the stalk is often thrown into the air. The useless chaff is blown away and the wheat remains.

But Jesus has prayed that Peter's faith will not be blown away. He asks the Father that Peter's faith will remain strong during his upcoming test and that, after stumbling, he'll return to strengthen others.

Notice Peter steps out in his own strength, using the big word "I." "Lord, with You I am ready to go both to prison and to death" (22:33). If we try to serve God, remain faithful to Him using only our own strength, we're in trouble. Jesus points out that no amount of willpower, no amount of Peter's power, will help him.

Finally, Jesus reminds the disciples how well they have been received by the world. Hospitality has been so great that they didn't even need extra shoes or a wallet. But now all of that's going to change. They must prepare themselves as if they're going into battle. Jesus makes the point clear by using the symbolism of buying a sword.

But the disciples misunderstand as usual. They take Him literally and show Him the two swords they have. For now Jesus doesn't try to straighten them out. But later, in the garden of Gethsemane, He scolds Peter for using a sword: "Put your sword back into its place; for all those who take up the sword shall perish by the sword" (Matthew 26:52).

A Fierce Battle

Day 6   *Read Luke 22:39-44*

Jesus goes off to pray by Himself after telling the apostles to pray that they won't give in to temptation. Things are going to get pretty rough for them these next few days, and they'll crumble if they try to rely on their own strength. They need God's help.

And now comes one of the fiercest and most important battles in all of history. Who will own earth? If Jesus refuses to die on the cross (which He can do), Satan will continue to rule the world. Man sold himself into slavery in the Garden of Eden. But if Jesus goes through with His sacrifice, the purchase, He will buy man back.

The fate of the entire world hangs in balance.

To be utterly and completely cut off from the Father after having a continual lifelong relationship with Him—to suffer all of the pain, all of the agony that otherwise would be ours—to have never sinned and suddenly find the sins of the world piled up on top of Him—this is what Jesus agrees to go through.

Granted, He is God the Son; but He also has to go through all the temptations man faces. And, inside, the man part of Him is screaming with agony as Satan begins applying his full pressure. This is Satan's chance; he's now fighting for his hold on the world, using everything in his power, his full force, to weaken Jesus into quitting.

How easily God could go home and give us up to die. After all, we deserve it. He didn't sell us into bondage; we sold ourselves.

"Father, if Thou art willing, remove this cup from Me" (22:42). All hell must be rejoicing at this apparent victory. Jesus doesn't want to go through the sacrifice, the pain, and the sorrow.

But His love for us is even greater than fear of the hellish anguish. He completes the statement, saying, "Yet not My will, but Thine be done" (22:42).

The Arrest

Jesus returns from the battle with Satan, only to find the disciples asleep. We read they're sleeping because of their "sorrow" (22:45). Whenever we feel sorrow or pressure, Satan will do anything he can to prevent us from praying, from connecting up with our power source, even if it means putting us to sleep. But remember, in any temptation we can refuse Satan by asking Jesus to take care of him.

Judas arrives in a crowd that's come to arrest Jesus, steps forward, and kisses Jesus on the cheek. How hard it must be for Jesus. He knows what Judas is up to but meekly receives this kiss of death.

When the people in the crowd approach Jesus, Peter steps out but manages only to cut off the ear of the high priest's slave. Again we see our weakness when we try to do things on our own. In trying to defend Jesus and fight off a whole crowd, Peter manages only to cut off somebody's ear. When we attempt to do things on our own, even though we think we're trying to do God's will, we often fail miserably.

Jesus gives Peter a tongue-lashing and immediately heals the ear. How often God comes back and patiently fixes what we've messed up.

Jesus points out the illegal manner in which He's being arrested as they lead Him away to the high priest's house. Peter and John follow at a distance.

In the courtyard of that house, Peter is accused

146

three times of being one of Jesus' followers; and three times he denies Him just as Jesus had said he would. What bitter heartache Peter must feel when on that third denial Jesus actually turns around and looks directly at him. But keep in mind that this same man will become one of the world's greatest Christian leaders. No matter how we've disappointed God in the past, He will still use us for great things if we allow Him.

At daybreak Jesus is brought before the Sanhedrin (the top religious leaders of the country). They ask if He's the Christ. He says they won't believe Him even if He tells them. They ask again. He says, "Yes, I am" (22:70).

They don't believe Him.

WEEK 12

The Compromise

Day 1   *Read Luke 23:1-12*

The members of the Sanhedrin still fear what the people may think, so they make sure the arrest takes place early in the morning before the rest of the city is awake. The Sanhedrin has no power to put a man to death and must take Jesus to the Roman governor, Pilate.

The hatred these "religious" men have for Jesus is so intense that they actually start lying in order to accuse Him. Jesus has never attempted to mislead the nation; He didn't forbid paying taxes (in fact He actually encouraged them to—"render to Caesar the things that are Caesar's" [Matthew 22:21]); and His claims of being King referred to the spiritual kingdom, not an earthly one.

Pilate also sees the Sanhedrin's lies and, after privately questioning Jesus, returns with the verdict: not guilty.

There it is: the official, legal verdict. The trial is over, and Jesus is found innocent and should be released.

But the people continue to complain and continue to lie. And Pilate, though he knows the right thing to do, begins to weaken. His fear of what people may think of him makes him change his mind on what he knows is right. Today, how many people don't do what they know is right for this same reason?

Though Jesus has been found innocent, He once again is forced to appear before Herod, King of the region Jesus is from.

Now Herod (the same one who had John beheaded) is pretty excited about Jesus' visit. He's been waiting a long time to see some miracles. He tries to pressure Jesus into performing a few but has no luck. It never crosses his mind to listen to Jesus and to take Him seriously.

Jesus knows Herod's motives and will not play his game. He remains quiet, fulfilling the prophecy in Isaiah 53:7: "He was oppressed, and He was afflicted, yet He did not open His mouth; like a lamb that is led to slaughter and like a sheep that is silent . . . He did not open His mouth."

Herod can't find Jesus guilty either, so after mocking and ridiculing Him, he returns Him to Pilate. Once again God has given Pilate the chance to accept what he already knows to be the truth and to do the right thing.

Pilate's Last Chance

Read Luke 23:13-31

Again Pilate calls for the chief priests, rulers, and people. Again he says he has found "no guilt" in Jesus. But despite Jesus' innocence, Pilate has Him whipped 39 times just to keep the people happy. Still they're not satisfied.

Pressure continues to mount on Pilate as the people continually try to persuade him to do what he knows is wrong. (Sound familiar?) But wait. Maybe he's found a way out. Maybe he won't have to take a stand for Jesus. It's customary to release one prisoner for the Passover celebration. He'll release Jesus and everyone will be happy.

Not quite. The crowd would rather see a murderer released than God the Son. For the third time, Pilate cries out to the crowd that Jesus is innocent. But the people want to see Jesus die.

Now there's no place for Pilate to run. He must make a decision: his old life with its luxuries and reputation, or God and the Truth—the decision every person in the world must make.

Pilate fails. He listens to the world instead of receiving what he knows to be the Truth.

Jesus hasn't had any sleep for about 30 hours. Within this period He has taught in the temple, eaten Passover supper, gone through the spiritual battle in the garden, and has received beatings and 39 lashes. He's so weak that someone else has to carry His cross.

Despite the overwhelming fatigue and pain, Jesus still has compassion and sympathy for the people.

Jesus tries to warn the women that things will get rough, very rough. It will be so bad that people will actually ask for the mountains to fall on them. Again it seems that Jesus is referring to the disaster that will shortly come on Jerusalem as well as the future calamity of the world.

How hard it must be for Jesus' followers to understand what the events of the last few days mean. Here's a man who claims to be the King, but He emphasizes that He didn't come to set up a political kingdom. Instead, He says His Father has sent Him to help prepare a heavenly kingdom. And now, as this man who says He's God is being dragged off to be killed, He is telling everyone about how tough the future is going to be.

None of this seems to make any sense to His followers. But they are in for the surprise of their lives.

"Into Your Hands"

Day 3

Read Luke 23:32-46
Psalm 22:1-18
Isaiah 53

This is one of history's most important moments. Since it is the key to whether man lives or dies, it is only natural for God to refer to it throughout the Old Testament. We could spend days studying the hundreds of prophecies on the subject, but for now let's look briefly at Psalm 22:1-18 (Jesus' view of His death) and Isaiah 53.

In just these two sections alone, we see many accurate predictions: the sneering and taunts, the appearance of His disjointed body, the heavy perspiration, His thirst, His pierced hands and feet, the casting of lots for His clothes, His death among criminals, His final words, all of the various aspects of His agony.

Yet, with all of that pain and suffering for the sins of the world, Jesus is still concerned for the well-being of others. He asks John to care for His mother (John 19:25-27); He forgives the criminal on the cross beside Him and promises him eternal life (Luke 23:43). He actually calls out to ask the Father to forgive those who are killing and mocking Him! (23:34) That's some love.

Suddenly the sun goes dark for three hours. That's too long for an eclipse. The earth begins to shake violently.

Finally Jesus cries out, "Father, into Thy hands I commit My spirit" (23:46). The temple curtain, the thick veil that symbolized the separation between man and God, is completely torn from top to bottom. No longer is man separated from God by his sins. Finally, after hours of suffering, God has paid for the world's sins. The sacrifice, the substitution for our punishment for our disobedience, is complete. Jesus finishes all that He came to do. The mission is accomplished. We're free. The tremendous debt that each of us has run up in heaven has been paid by another—in full.

Satan has lost. The war is over. Now it's simply up to each of us to step forward and claim the victory that has already been won for us.

The Burial

The centurion is the captain in charge of the soldiers who have put Jesus to death. He's seen the grisly affair through from the beginning. And this tough, rugged soldier breaks into praises to God as he recognizes Jesus as the Son of God.

Crucifixions are the sadist's joy in life, and there's a large crowd on hand for this one. But instead of being entertained as they have hoped for, they leave upset after seeing all that has happened.

Two members of the Sanhedrin, Joseph of Arimathea and Nicodemus (secret followers of Jesus), are willing to risk persecution from their friends and ask Pilate for permission to bury the body (John 19:38-40). They use Joseph's tomb, the one he had been planning to use for himself. As a result we see another prophecy (Isaiah 53:9) being fulfilled: "His grave was assigned to be with wicked men, yet with a rich man in His death."

There is very little time left before sundown (before the Sabbath begins), so they wrap the body and lay it in the tomb.

Nowhere do we read of Peter's presence or of those who were so boastful about their allegiance to Jesus. Instead, the ones who are barely mentioned by name do what God asks without hoping to be in the spotlight.

"He Is Not Here,
but He Has Risen"

Day 5   *Read Luke 24:1-12*

Luke often gives just the bare facts without including many of the details. But by combining the Book of Luke with some of the other Gospels, we begin to get a fuller picture.

The body has been placed in a tomb, a large hole chiseled out of rock with a gigantic stone rolled across the opening. On the request of the Pharisees and the chief priests, Pilate has agreed to station about 10-30 guards around the tomb to prevent anyone from stealing the body.

As the women approach the tomb to finish the embalming, they begin worrying about who might move the stone for them. But when they arrive, they find things slightly different from the way they had expected. The stone has been rolled away by an angel; the guards are in a state of shock ("like dead men" [Matthew 28:4]); and a couple angels begin speaking to them.

They remind the women what Jesus said about rising on the third day. Of course! Suddenly all of Jesus' words begin to make sense. All of His mysterious sayings and puzzling statements begin to fit together.

They rush to tell the apostles the good news but are met with scoffing and unbelief. Still, Peter and John go to the tomb (just to make sure) and find it exactly as the women had said—completely empty except for the grave clothes neatly folded on one side. The men

rush off, leaving Mary Magdalene behind (John 20:
1-11). It is then that Jesus appears to her personally
(20:14-17).

Meanwhile, the chief priests are busy bribing the
guards to say they fell asleep at the tomb. The penalty
for sleeping while on guard duty is death, but the
leaders assure the soldiers that they'll make sure Pilate
takes no action against them.

Jesus Teaches a Bible Study

Day 6   *Read Luke 24:13-32*

Later that same Sunday, a couple disciples are heading toward another city. They're talking about all that has taken place when Jesus joins them, disguised in some way. He begins asking questions, testing them to find out how much they really understand about what has happened. The disciples stop and call the disguised Jesus a real dummy. "Are you the only one . . . unaware of these things?" (24:18) But Jesus plays along, asking the disciples to explain what has happened from their point of view.

They begin to describe Jesus only as a prophet. That must pain the Lord a little after all He has said and done, but He lets them continue. They were hoping He would free Israel. But three days ago He was killed, and now all of their dreams are smashed. And to make matters worse, some of the more respected women of the group are beginning to hallucinate, making up stories of how angels have supposedly talked to them.

Jesus finally sets them straight, pointing out how necessary it was *for us* that He suffer first. He then goes through all of the Old Testament prophecies that teach that the Messiah has to come and to suffer for our sins. (That must have been quite a lengthy Bible study, going through those hundreds of prophecies—even longer than this book.)

Imagine, having the Author of the Bible teaching it.

157

It must have been terrific to see Jesus, to listen to Him teach, to walk by His side, to talk with Him and ask questions. How much clearer everything would be, we think.

But that's not true. Back then, Jesus could only be at one place at one time. People had to go to that one place to reach Him. But we have something even better. Today each one of us (who has asked Him) actually has the Holy Spirit inside him, teaching and instructing. Jesus is no longer a person living on the outside we have to meet in the flesh to understand.

It's one thing to walk beside Jesus on a road but quite another to have His Spirit living inside us. Let's take advantage of that presence. When the Bible seems like it's boring or there's something we don't understand, let's take the time to ask the Holy Spirit to make it interesting, to make it clearer, to reveal more truth. Ask Him. The best Instructor in the universe lives inside each of us. We should ask Him—and not forget to wait for the answer. Plowing ahead alone, rushing through Scripture won't get us where we want to go. We should ask and wait.

"I Am with You Always"

After realizing Jesus was talking with them, the two disciples race to Jerusalem to tell the rest of His followers. They're busy filling the others in on all the details when suddenly Jesus appears.

They all become frightened, thinking He is a ghost. Jesus understands their fears and, to prove to them that He's not a ghost, that He's been physically resurrected from the dead, He tells them to touch Him.

Still the news seems too good to them, and they're afraid to believe it. Jesus again understands, and in His patience asks for some food to eat so they will know He has a physical body.

He then begins another study, explaining how the Old Testament prophecies were fulfilled by His suffering for us.

He continues to explain that repentance for forgiveness of sins must be proclaimed to the whole world, starting right there in Jerusalem. But they must not go out and tell the world about Him before they receive the power of the Holy Spirit.

During the next 40 days, Jesus makes several more appearances. At one time He appears to over 500 people.

Finally the time comes for Him to leave, to prepare a place for us and to send the Holy Spirit. He rises up into the clouds with the promise that He'll return in exactly the same way.

But remember, He's not gone. The Holy Spirit has been put inside each Christian; and every minute of every day if we let Him He'll continue to teach, protect, and above all, love. But only if we let Him.

Want to know about Him? Read all about Him in God's Book.